Geomantic Art

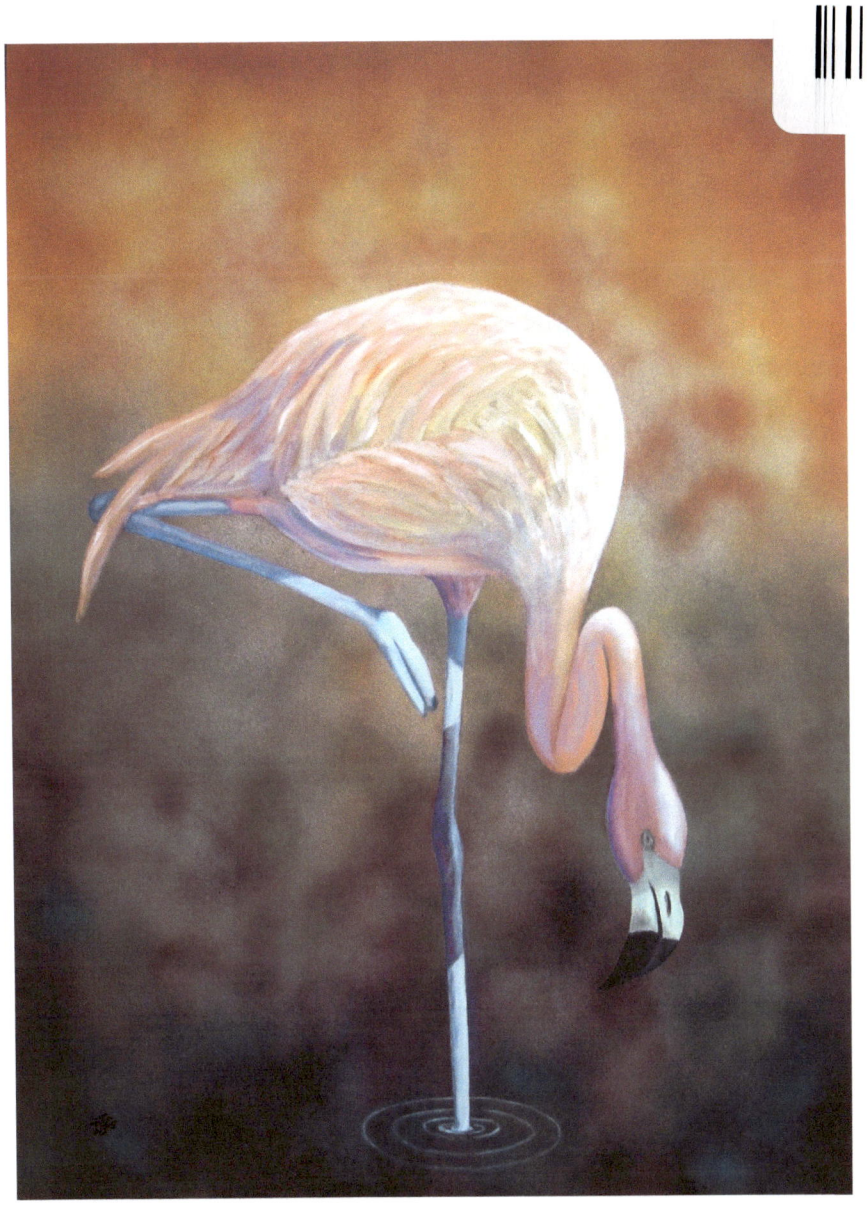

By Dr. David J. Goodwill

About the Artist

Dr. Goodwill was born in Liverpool and grew-up in post WW II England. He was educated in Oxford and then attended the University of Cambridge. He graduated from Cambridge at age 26 with a doctorate. He moved permanently to the USA in 1986 and is a US citizen.

Because his father was a high school art teacher and artist, Dr. Goodwill grew up surrounded by a wide variety of art and artistic imagery. From a young age, he exhibited artistic flair and talent. Art always remained his first love even though his career steered him in a different direction.

He spent much of his working life in corporate America, the last twenty years of which were as the CEO of divisions of large international corporations. Now he is able to return to his first love, art, and to concentrate on it full time

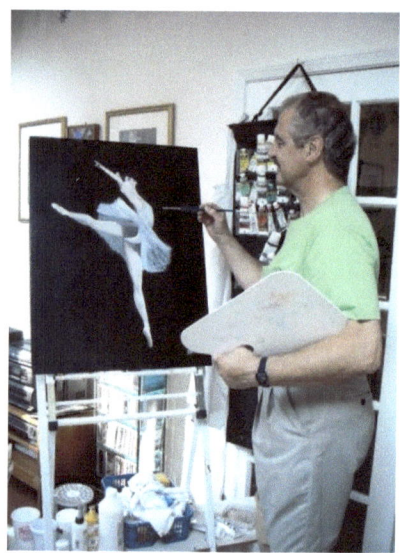

Artist's Statement

"Je peins donc je suis" …translation: I paint therefore I am. This is how I feel about art. It is a play on words after Rene Descartes, the famous French writer, who said, "Je pense donc je suis" (translation: "I think therefore I am"). There are painters and there are artists; I strive to be the latter. I use a style and medium that allows me to capture the subject. It is my view that the two areas of human endeavor that really matter in the long term are **art** and **science**. I have been fortunate to have delved seriously into both. I now choose to dedicate my energies to art.

Introduction

This book is a book of paintings by Dr. David J. Goodwill made during the last ten years. The theme running through his work is "Geomantic Art", a concept and term that he invented and is unique to his work.

Geomantic Art-Defined

The essential ingredients for a painting are <u>structure</u> and <u>content</u>. "Structure" describes the special characteristics or geometry of the picture; "content" the subject matter. Together they make up the composition.

Goodwill, the scientist, has shaped Goodwill, the artist. Fusing <u>geometry</u> with a preference for whimsical or <u>romantic</u> subjects gives rise to the term for this style: "<u>Geomantic</u>". Some pieces are purely geometric. In others the structure gives way to content, but the arrangement or position of objects and subject matter, and even the predominant colors used, are still governed by geometry.

The Geomantic methodology is the consistent and common theme throughout Goodwill's work.

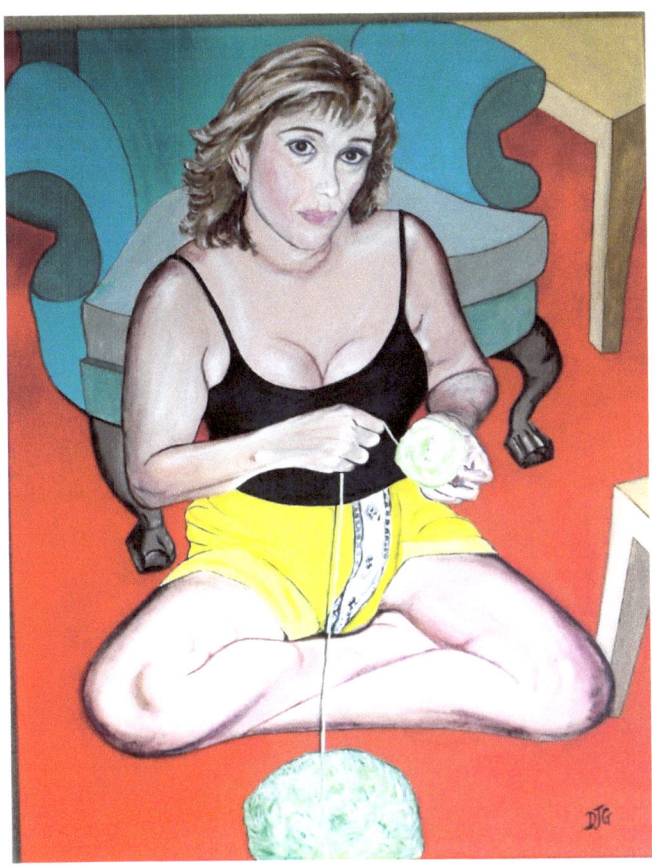

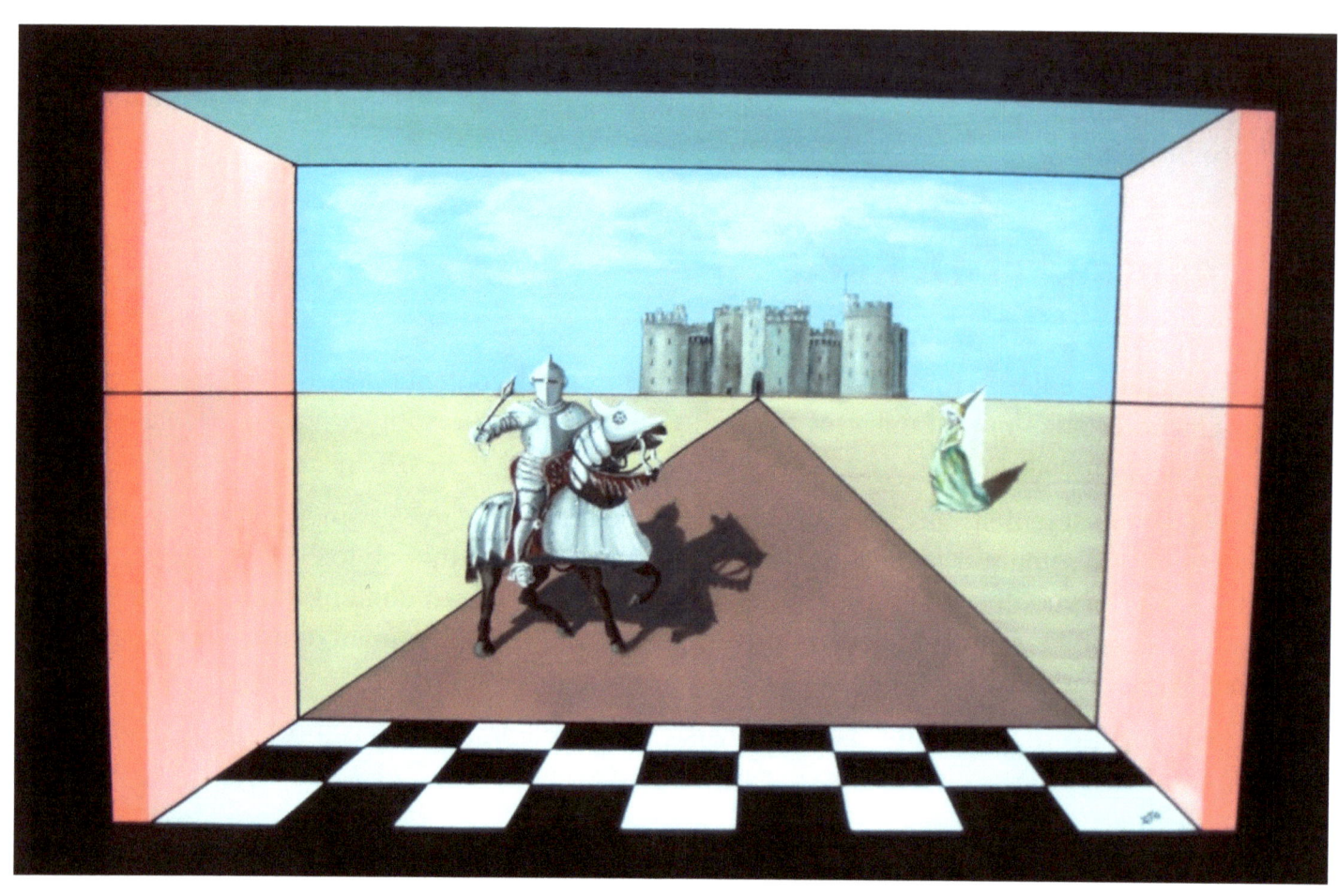

Whimsy 1 – Sir Knight -- Acrylic on canvas - 24" x 36

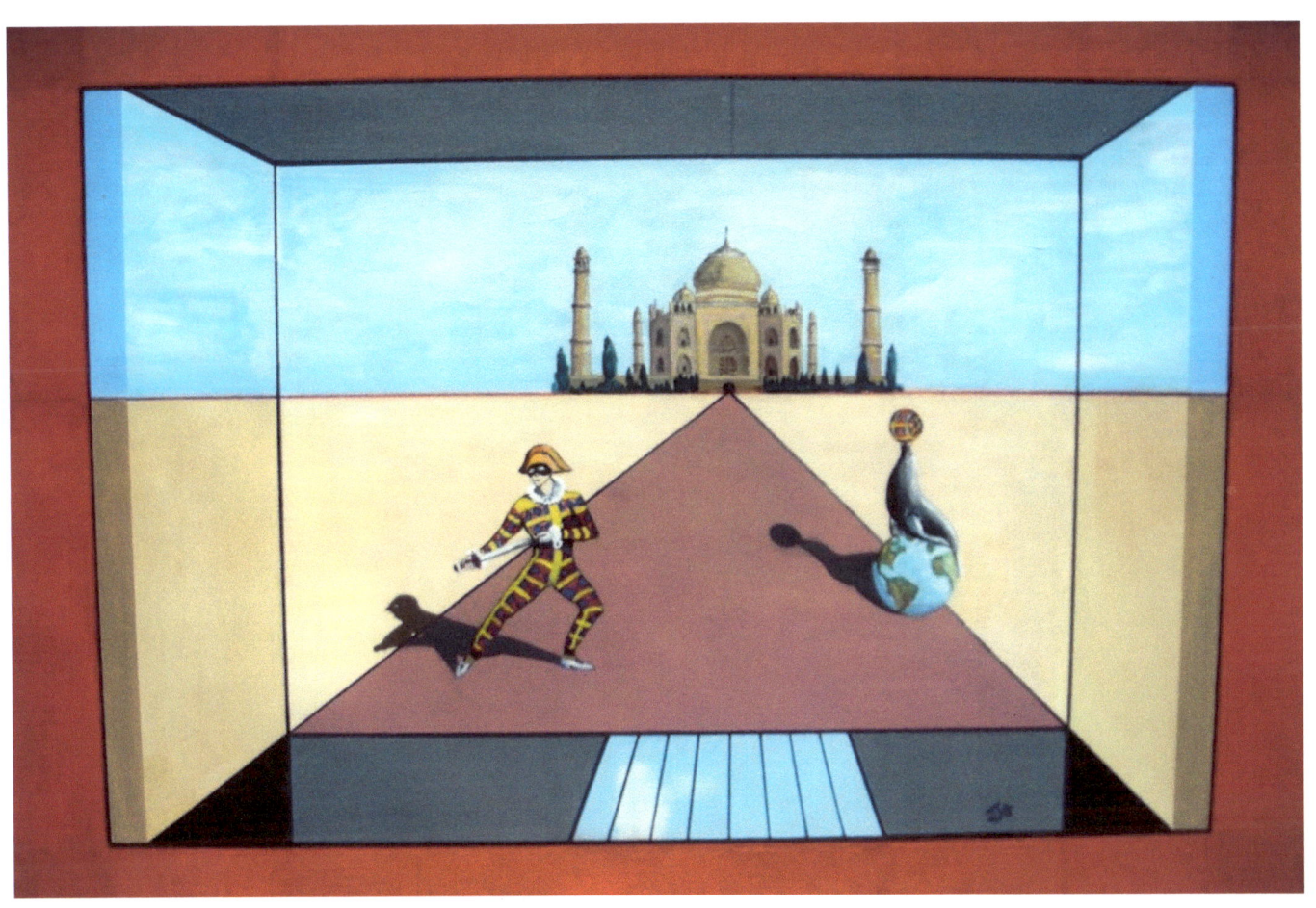

Whimsy 2 Harlequin -- Acrylic on canvas - 24" x 36"

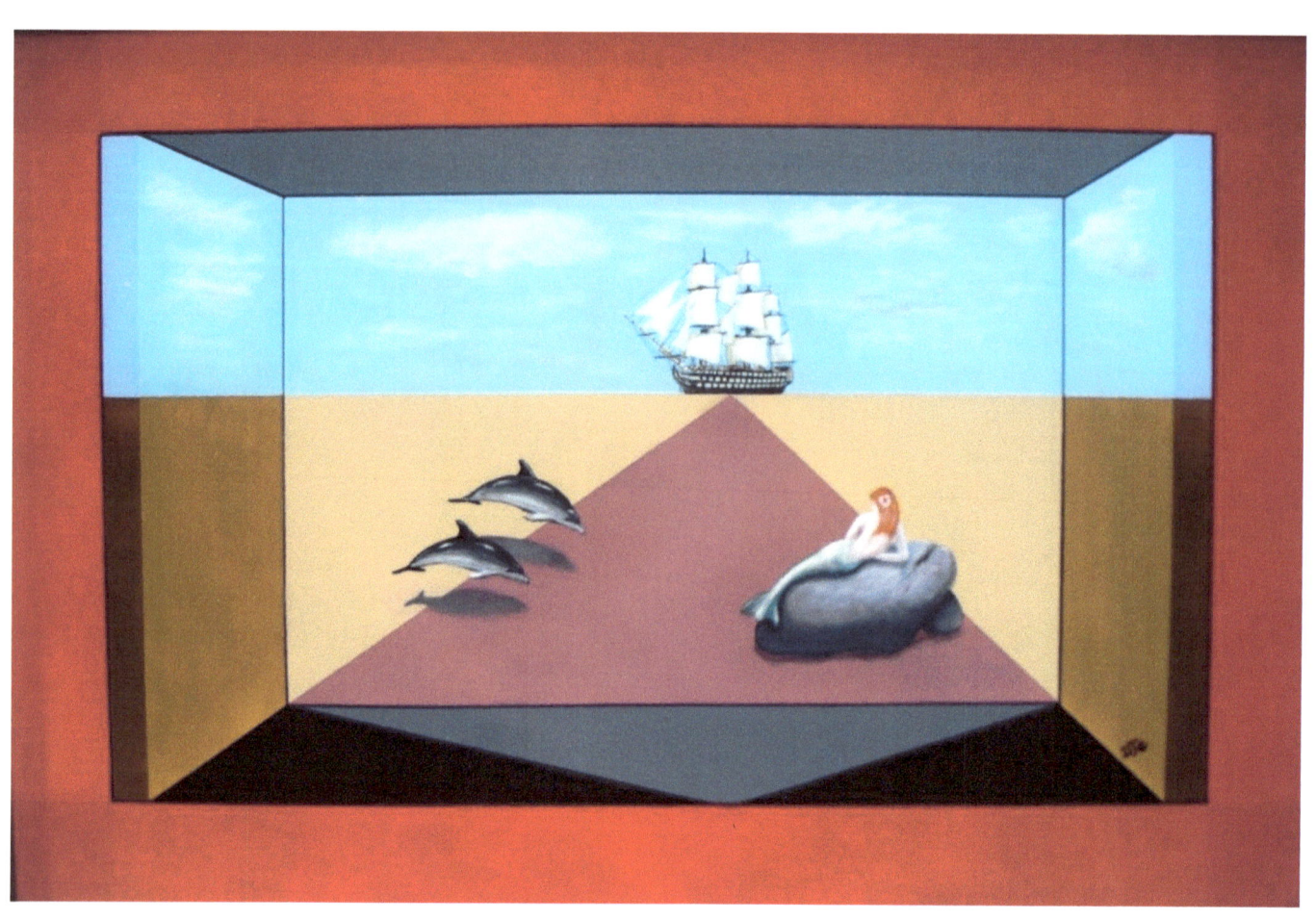

Whimsy 3 – Mermaid -- Acrylic on canvas - 24" x 36"

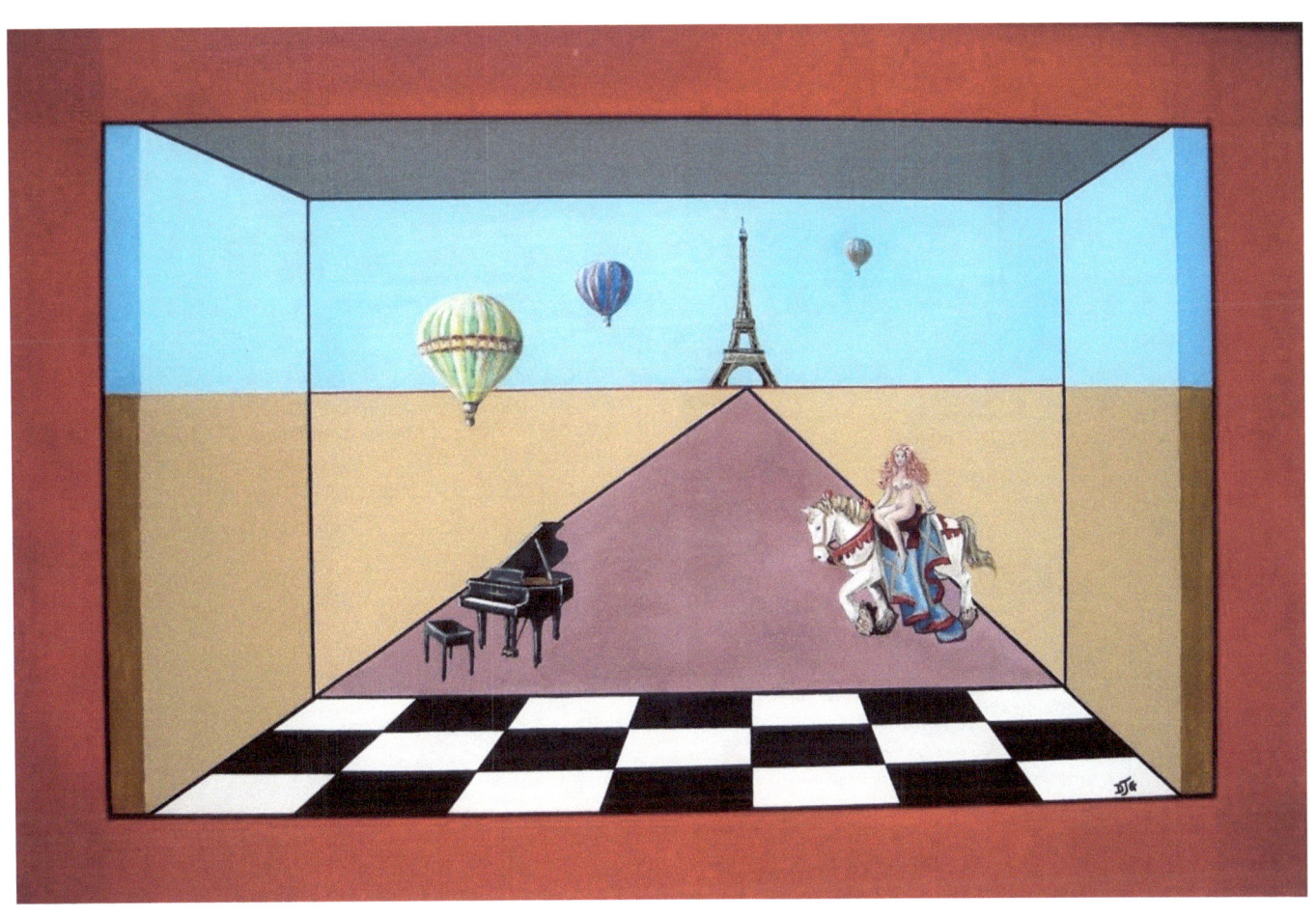

Whimsy 4 – Lady Godiva -- Acrylic on canvas - 24" x 36"

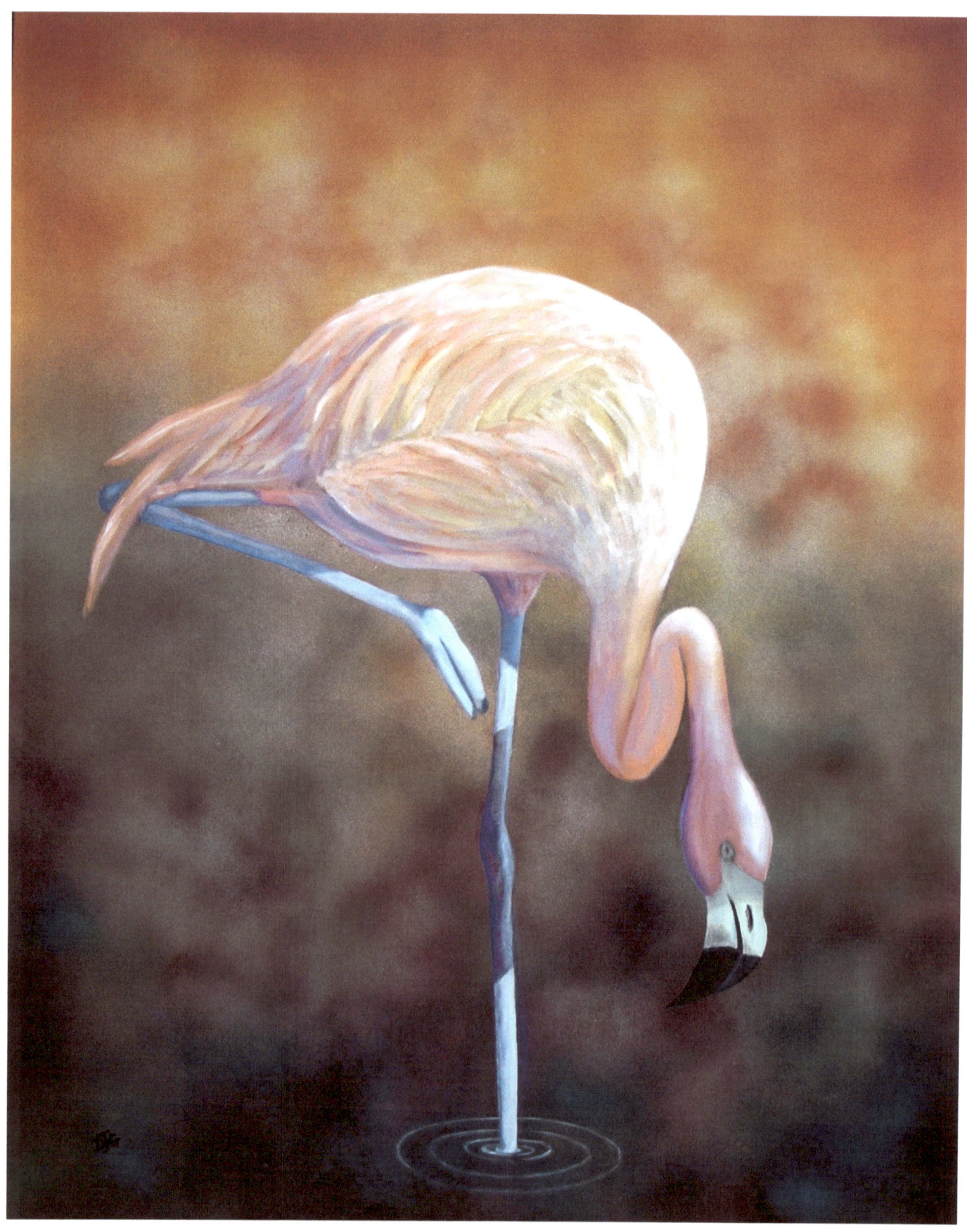

Flamingo -- Mixed Media on canvas - 36" x 48"

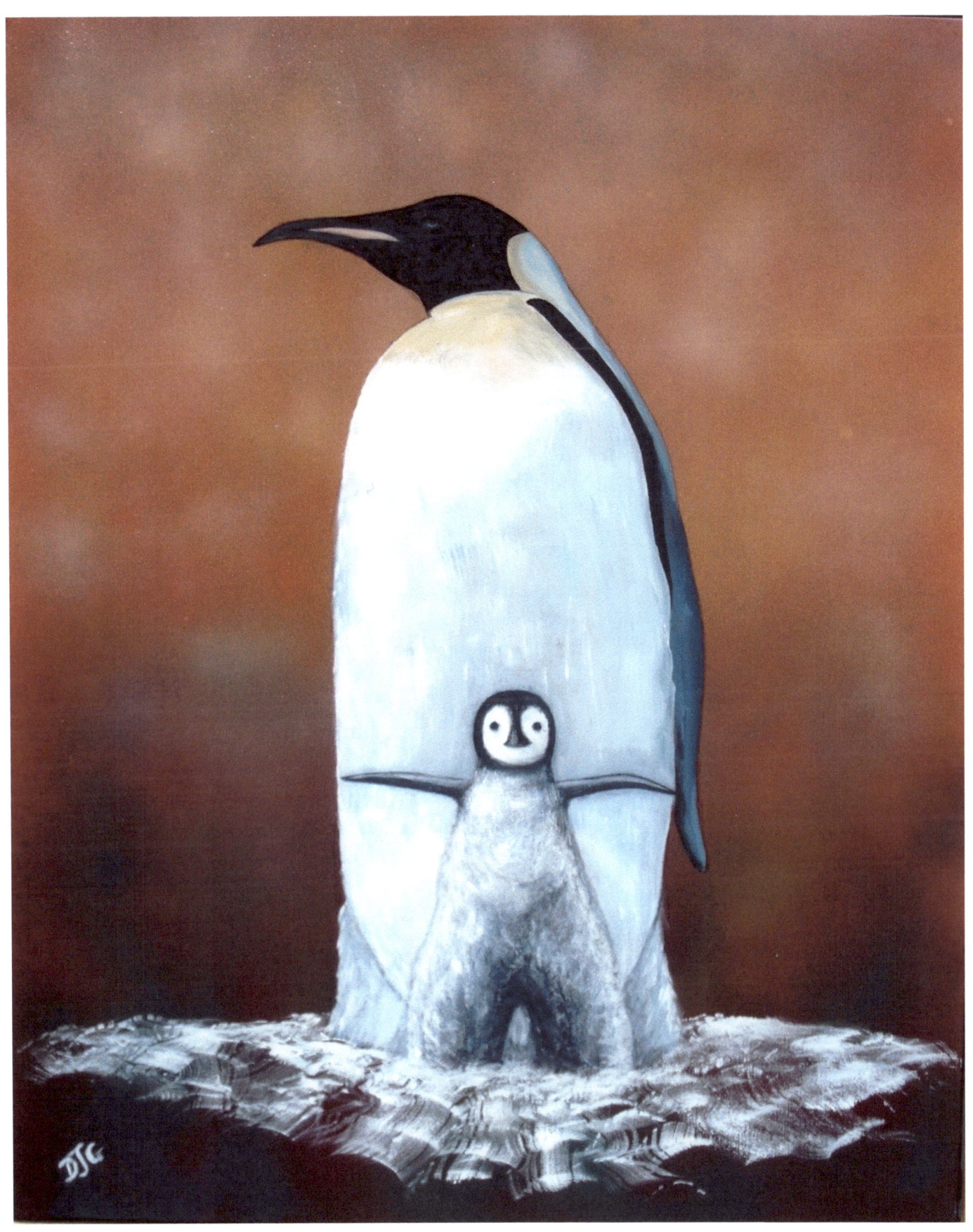

Penguins -- Mixed Media on canvas - 30" x 40"

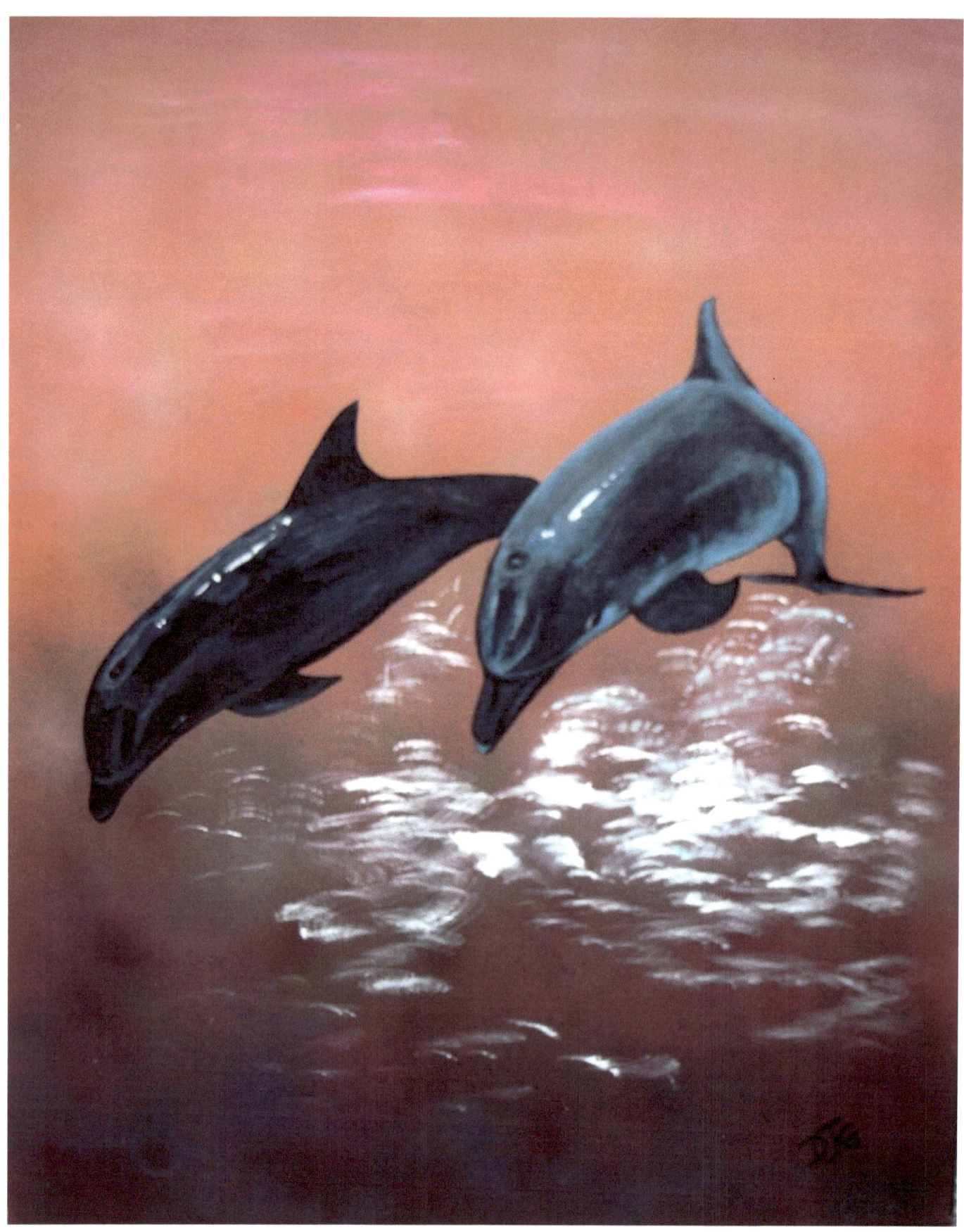

Dolphins -- Mixed Media on canvas - 30" x 40"

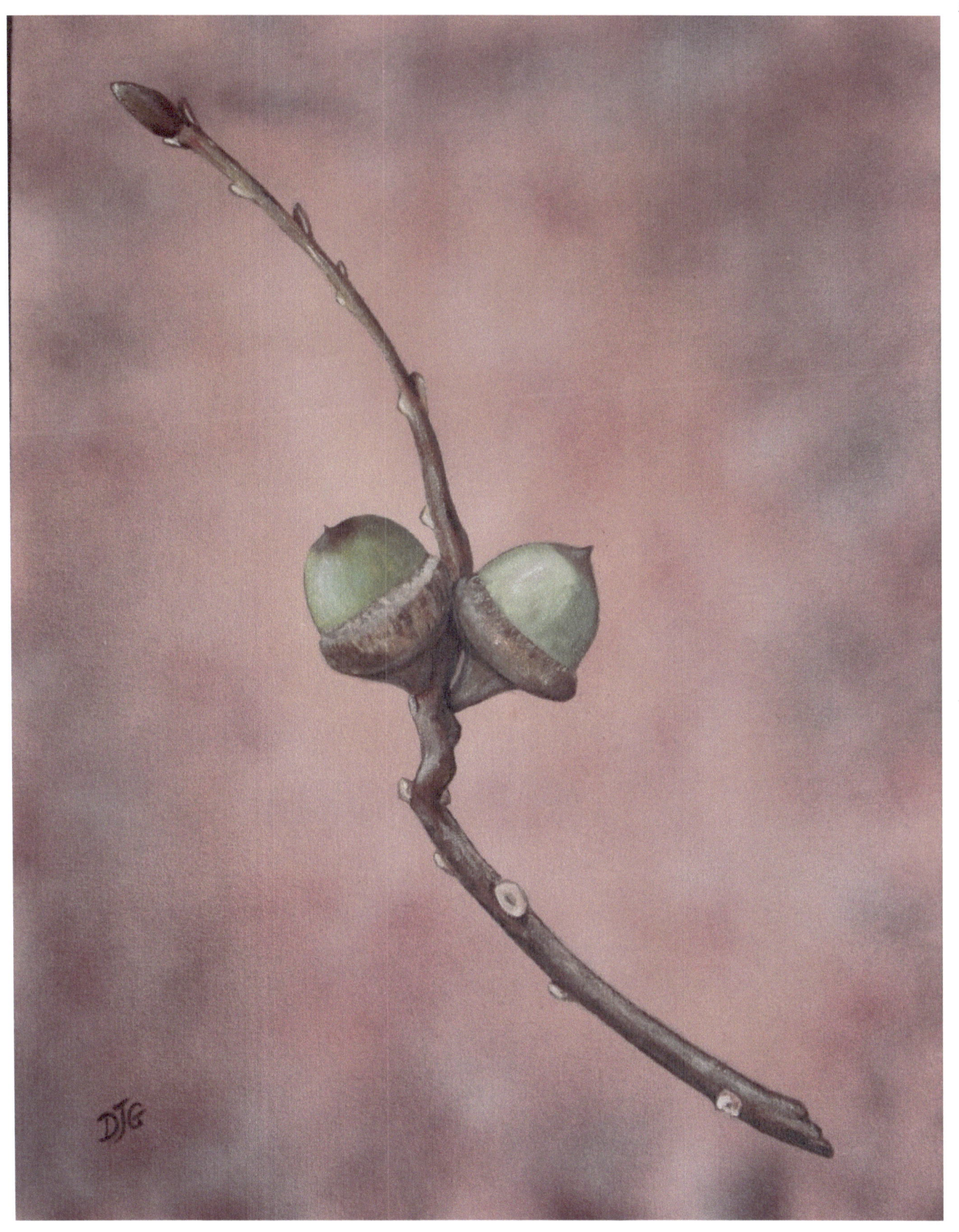

Oak Twig -- Mixed Media on canvas - 24" x 30"

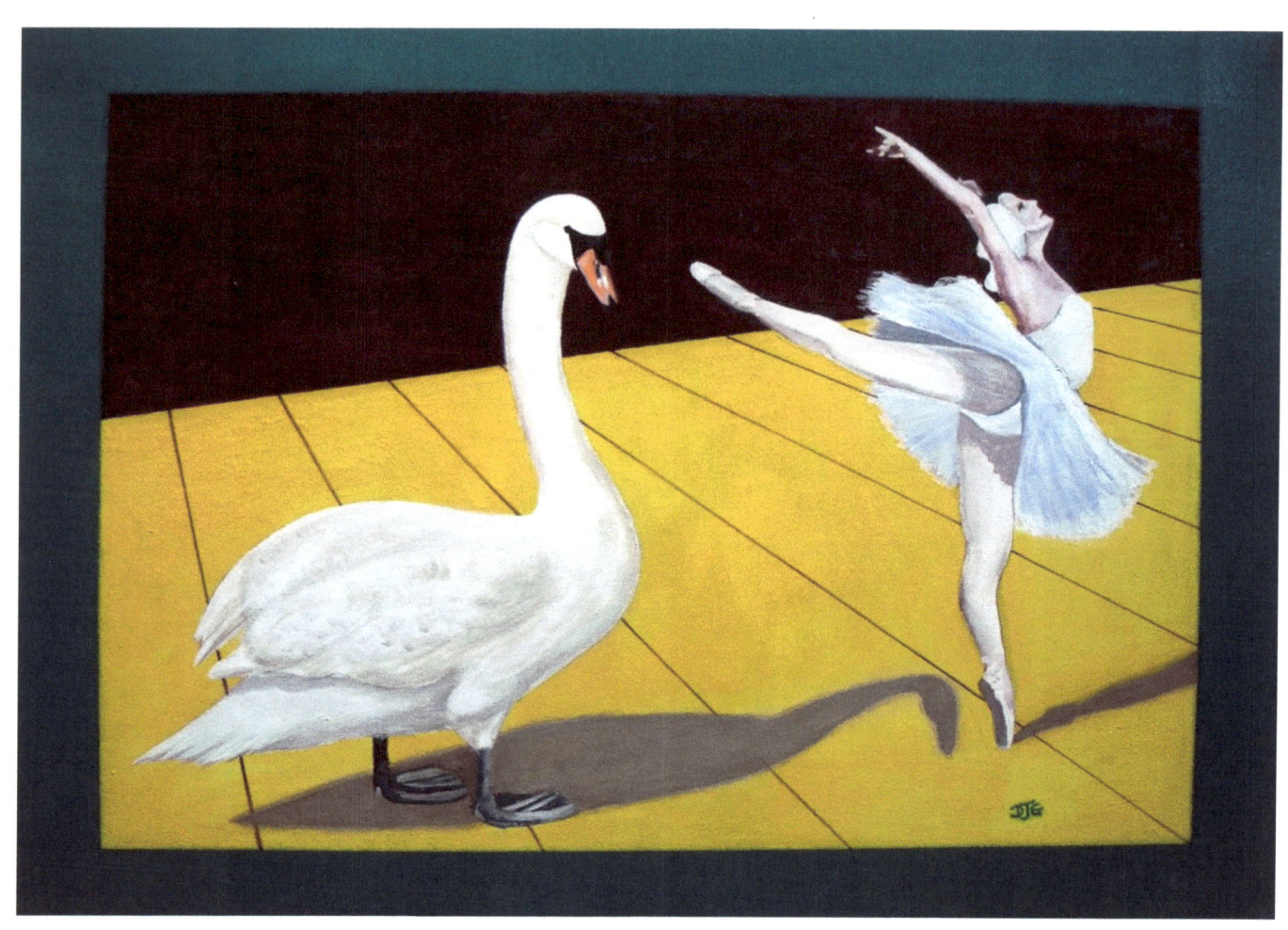

Swan Lake – Acrylic on canvas - 20" x 24"

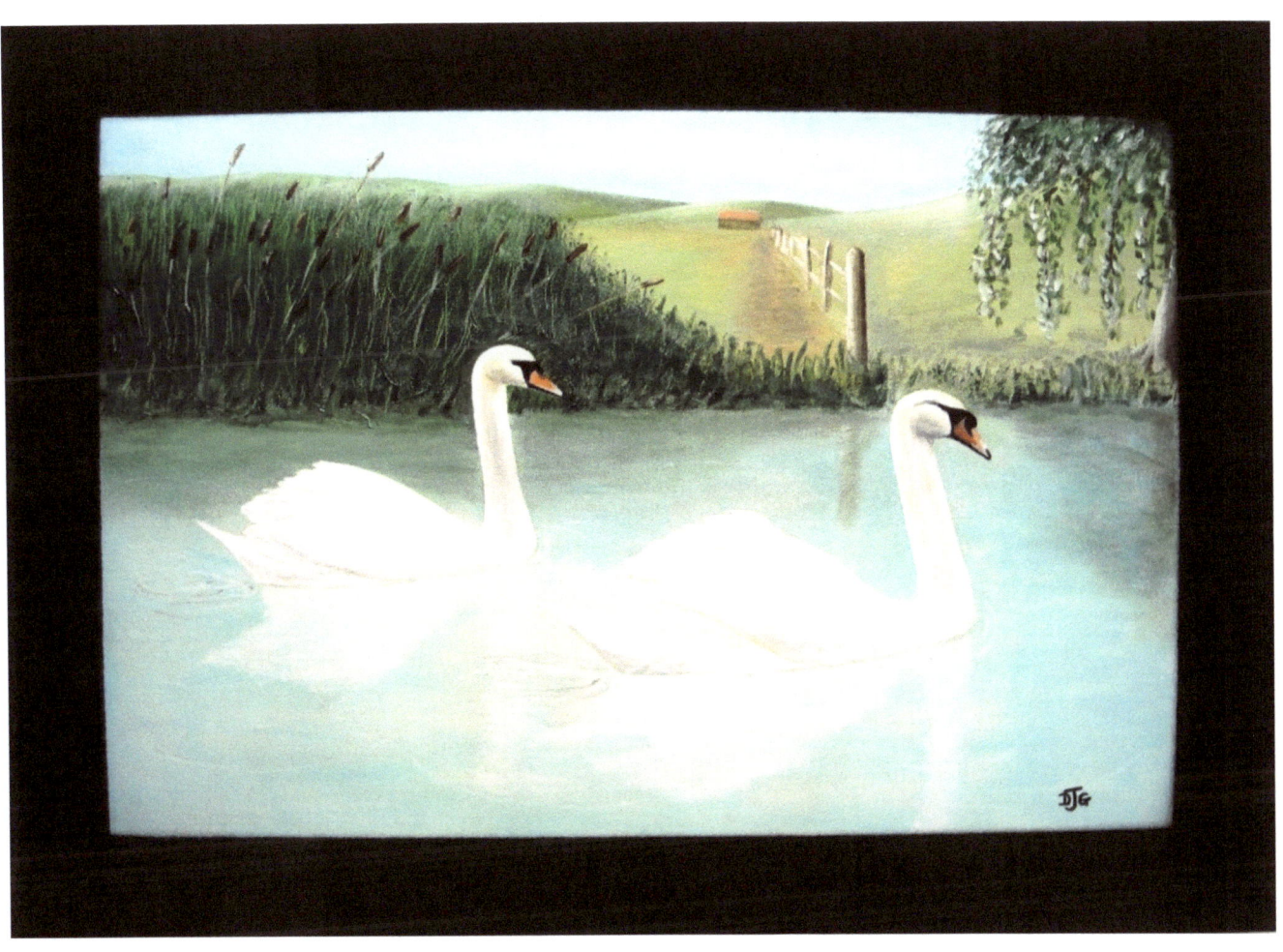

Swans -- Acrylic on canvas - 22" x 28"

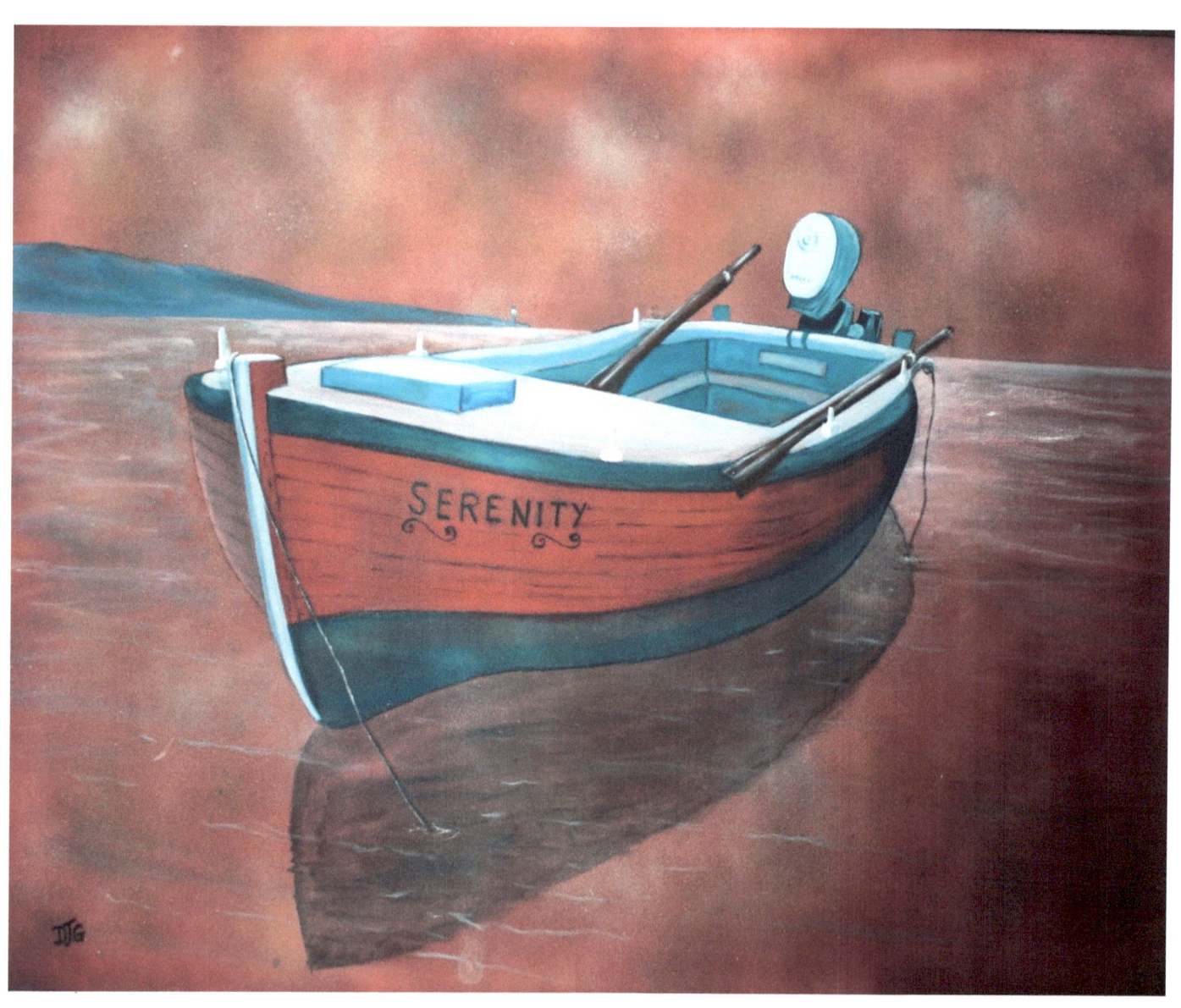

Serenity 1 -- Mixed Media on canvas - 30" x 40"

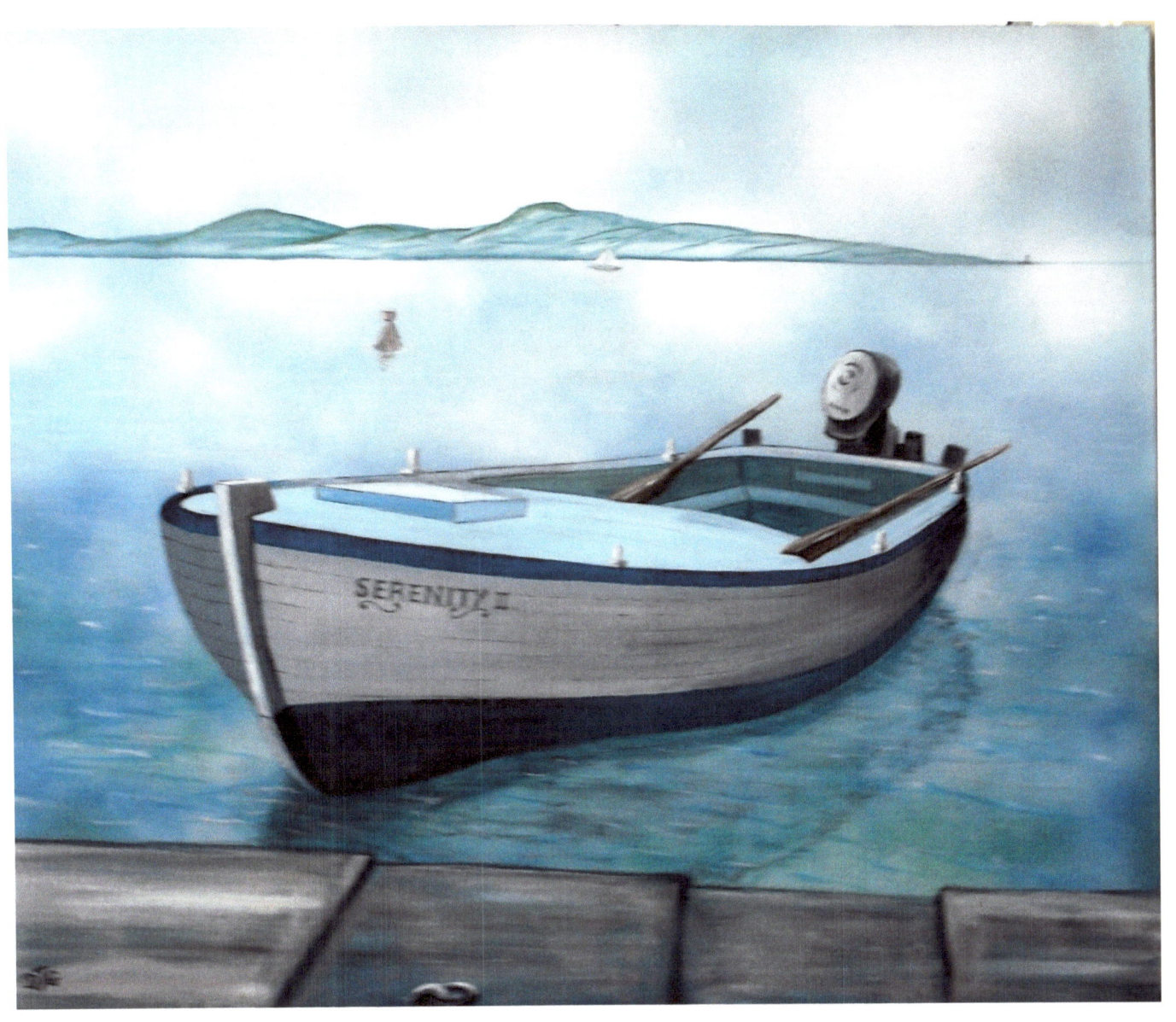

Serenity 2 -- Mixed Media on canvas - 36" x 36"

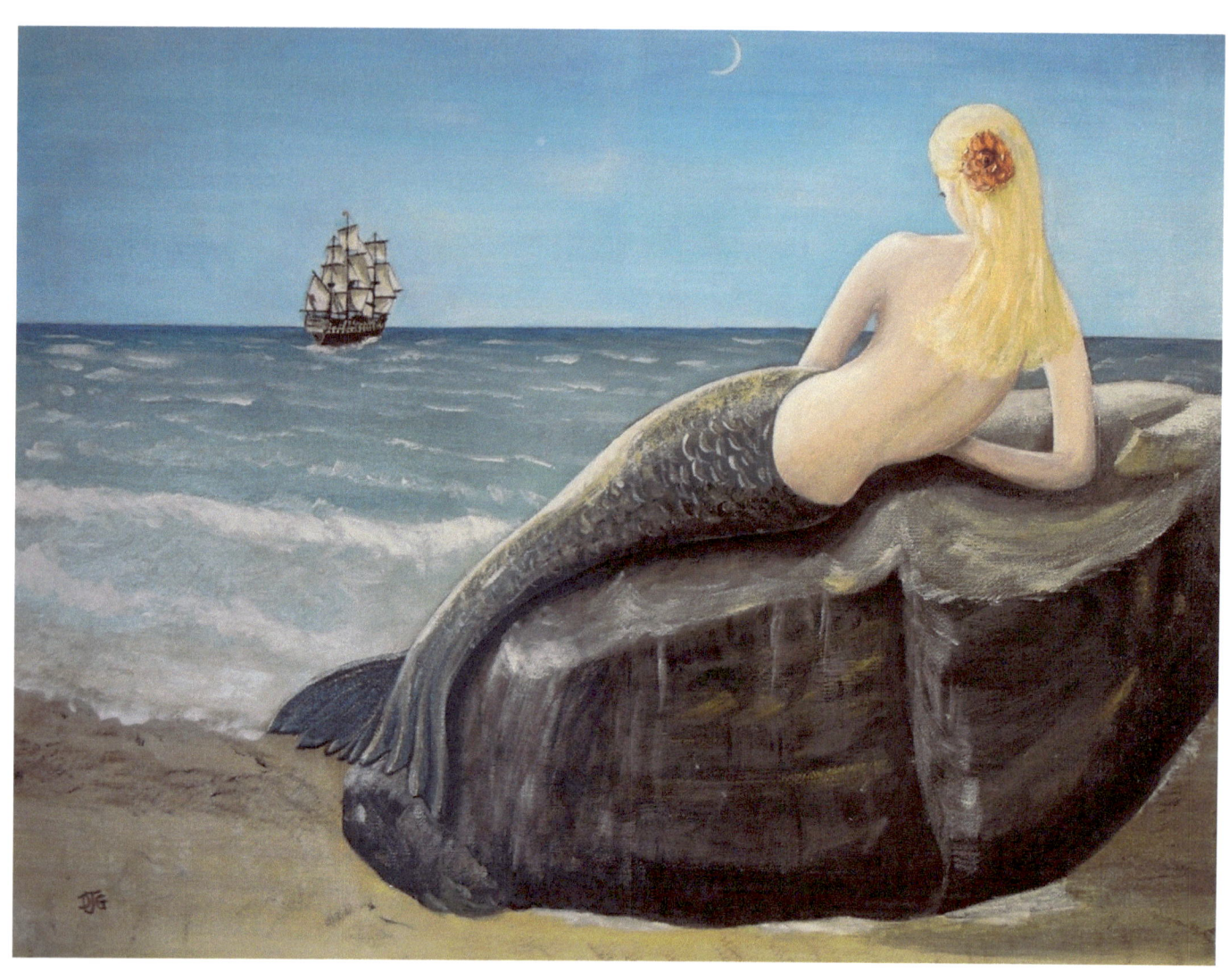

Parting is Such Sweet Sorrow – Acrylic on canvas – 24" x 30"

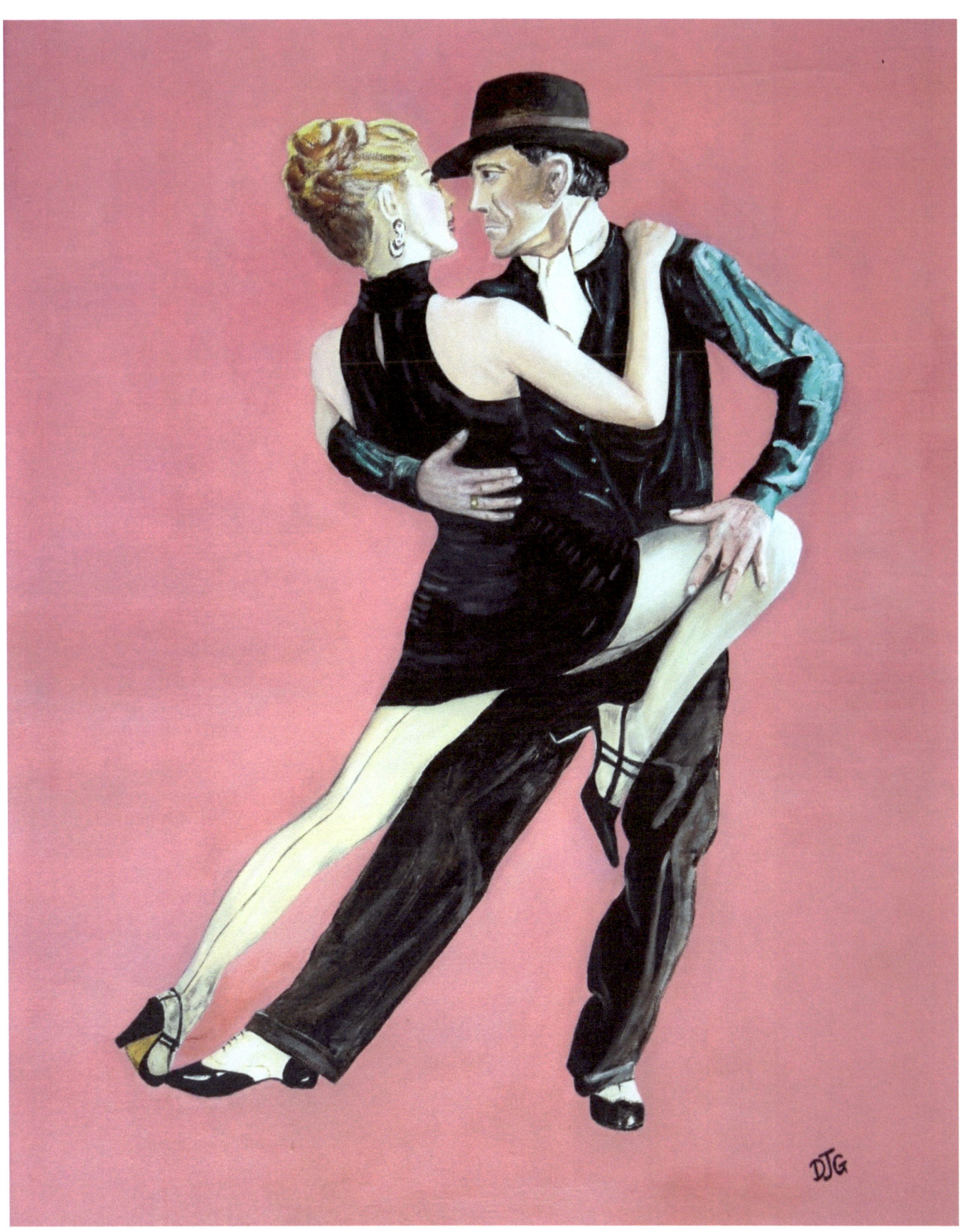

Tango Dancers -- Acrylic on canvas- 24" x 30"

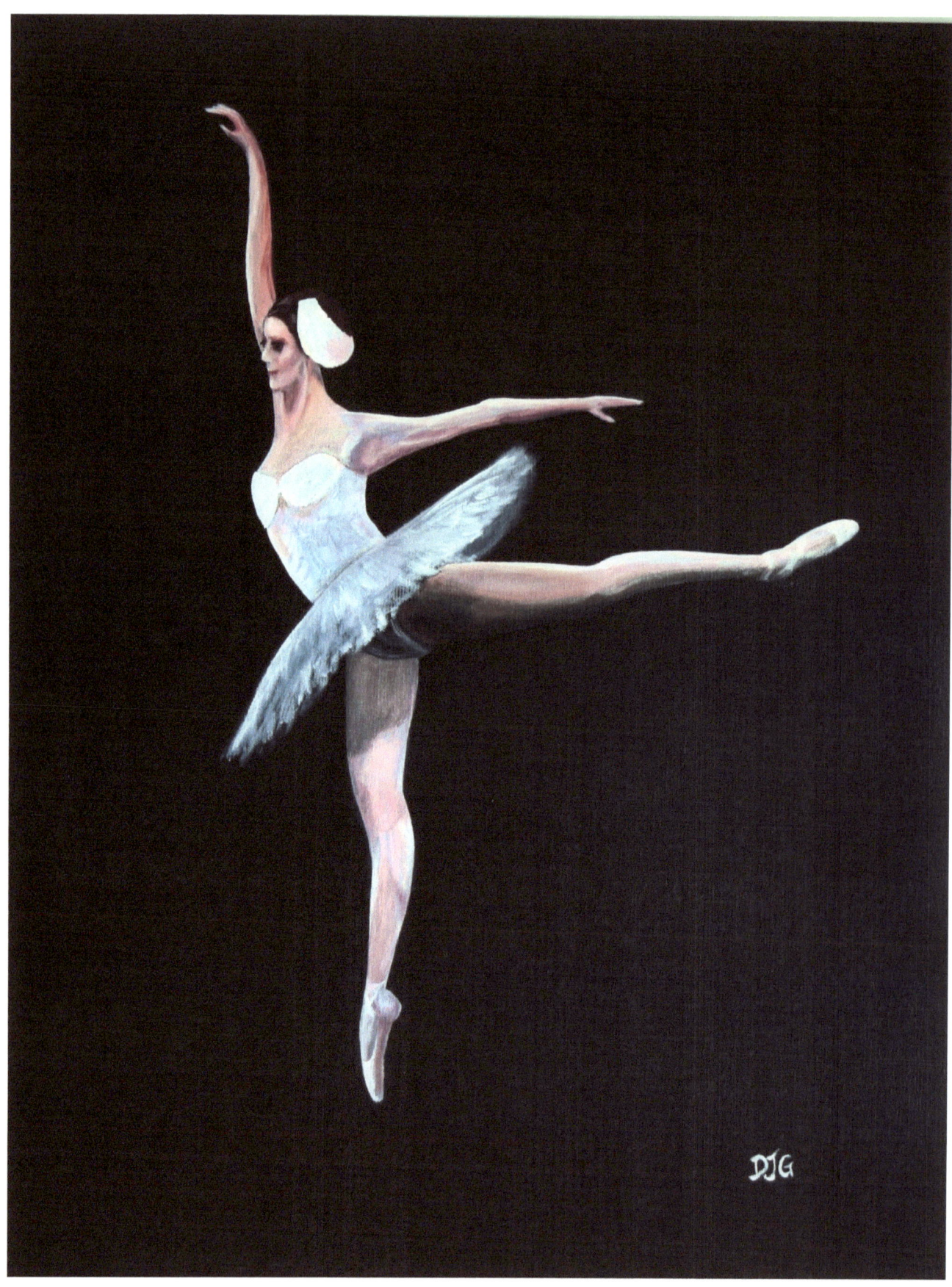

Ballerina 1 -- Acrylic on canvas - 24" x 30"

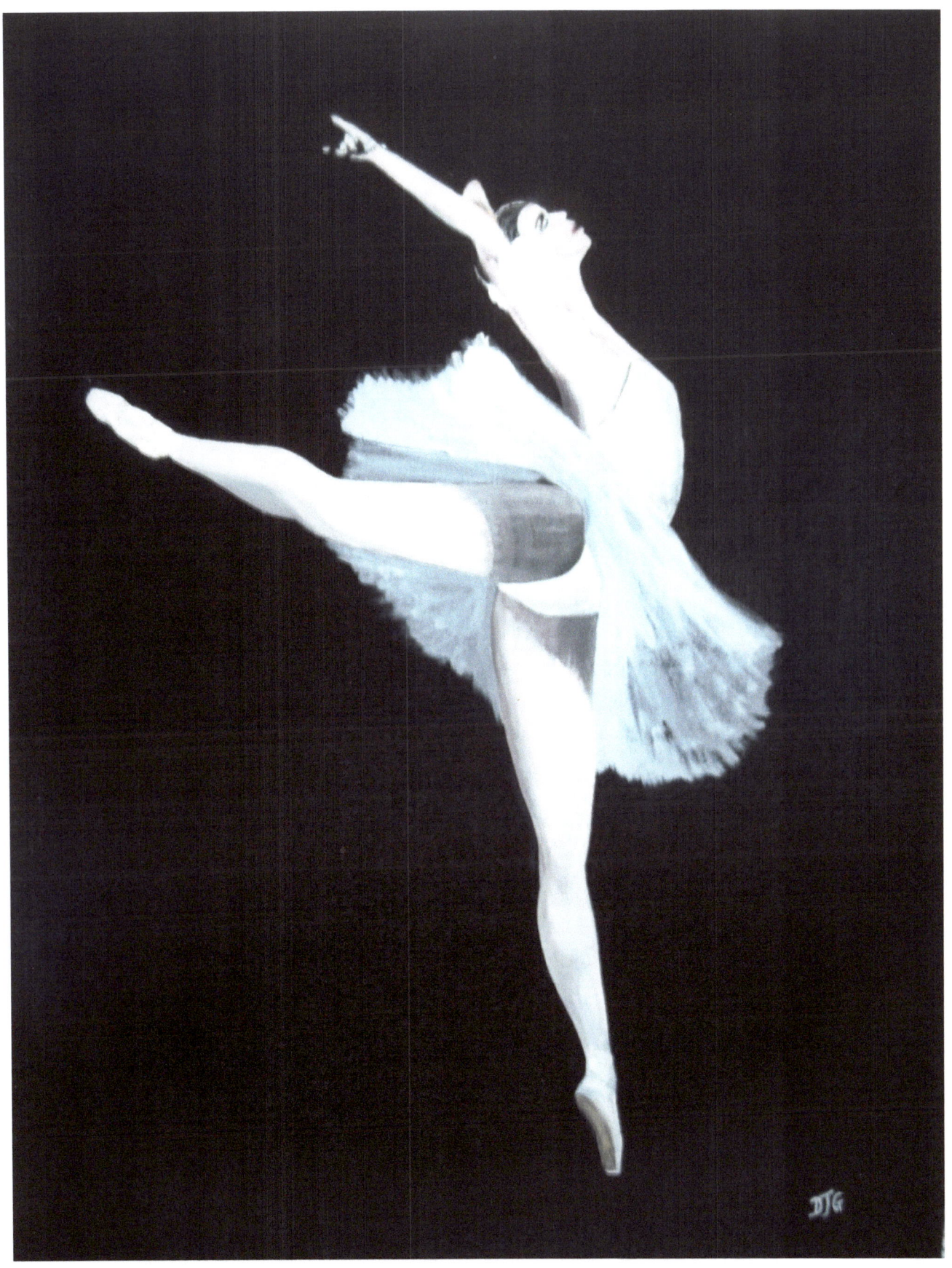

Ballerina 2 -- Acrylic on canvas - 24" x 30"

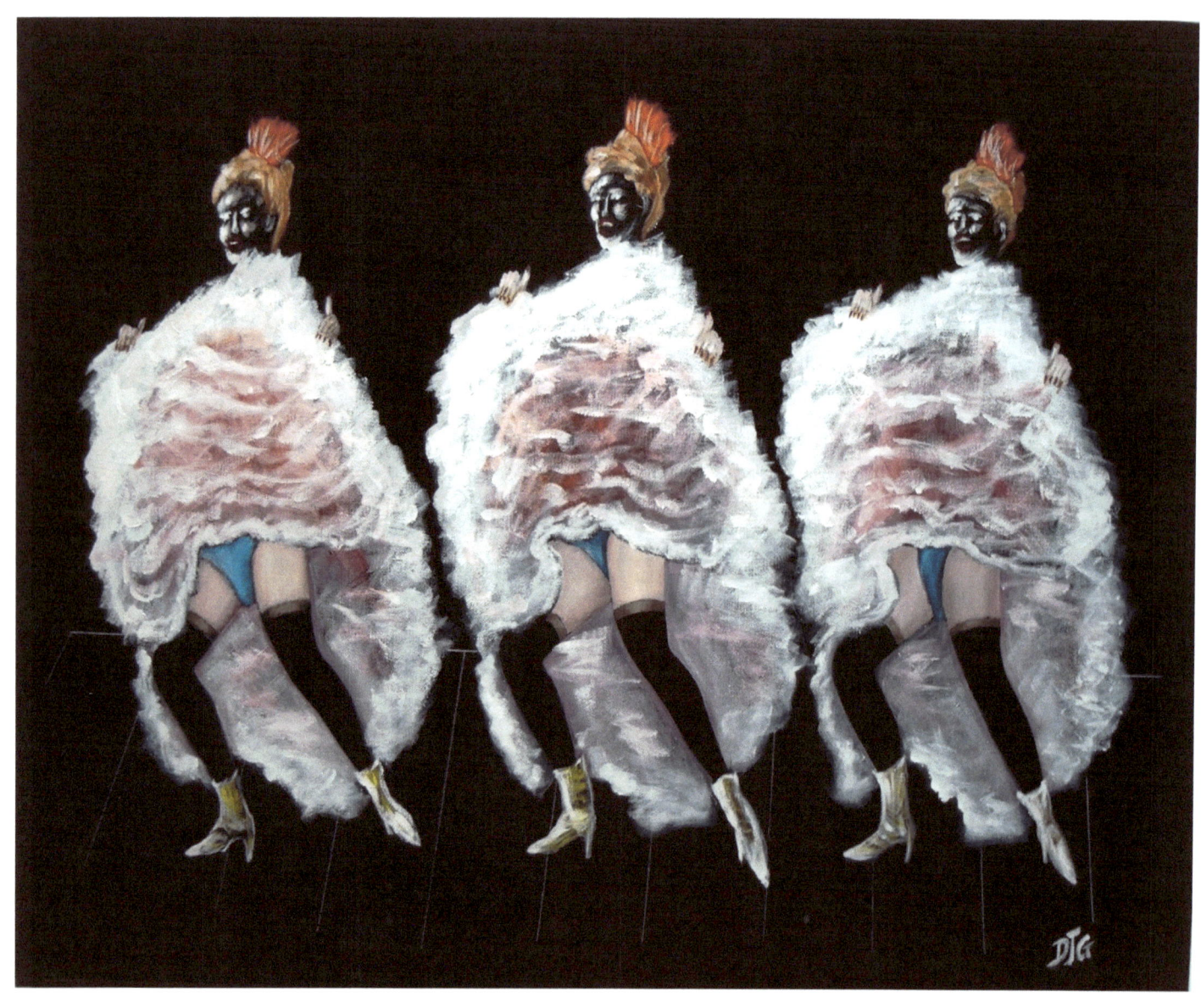

Can-Can Dancers 1 -- Mixed Media on canvas – 24" x 36"

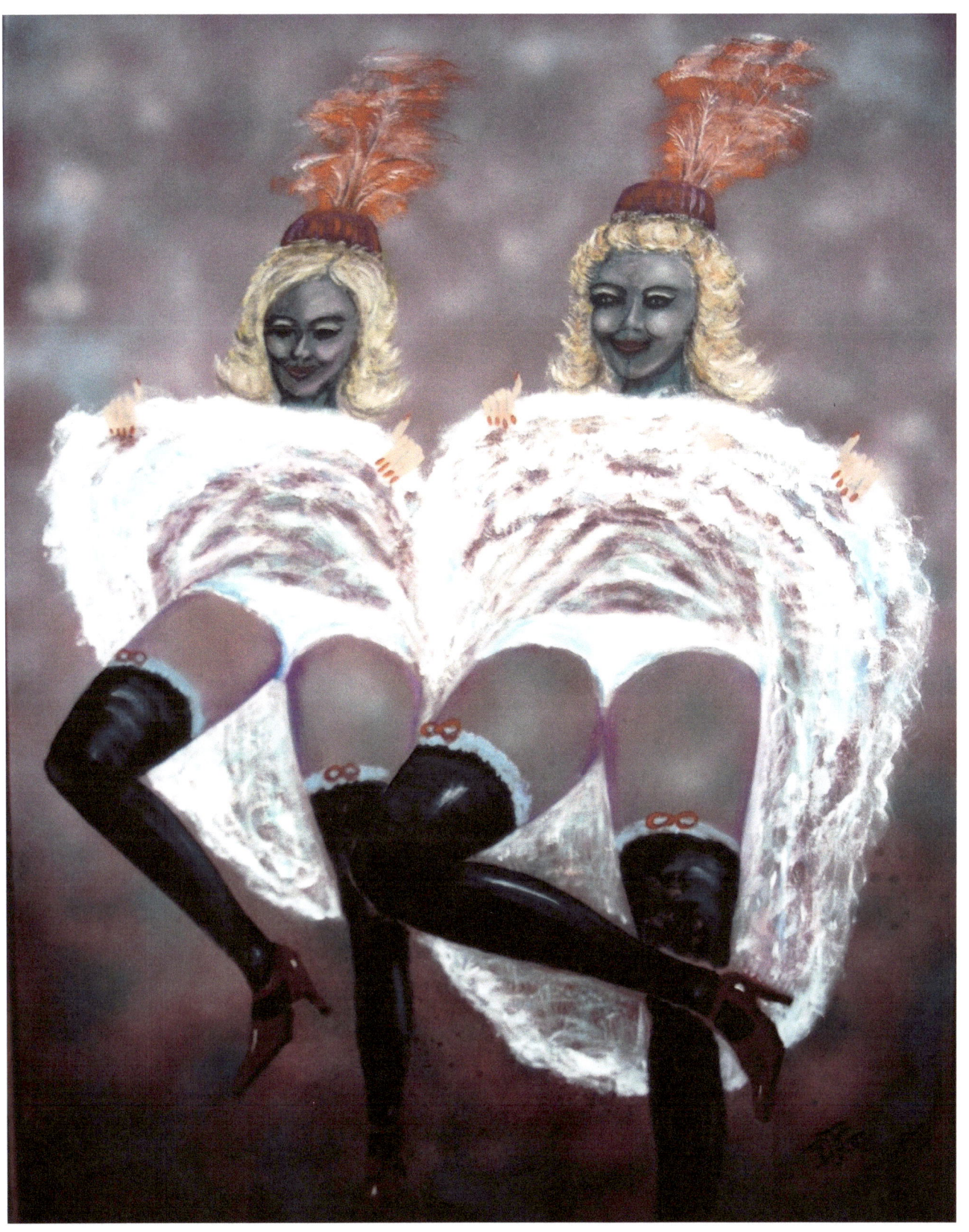

Can-Can Dancers 2 – Mixed Media on canvas – 36" x 48"

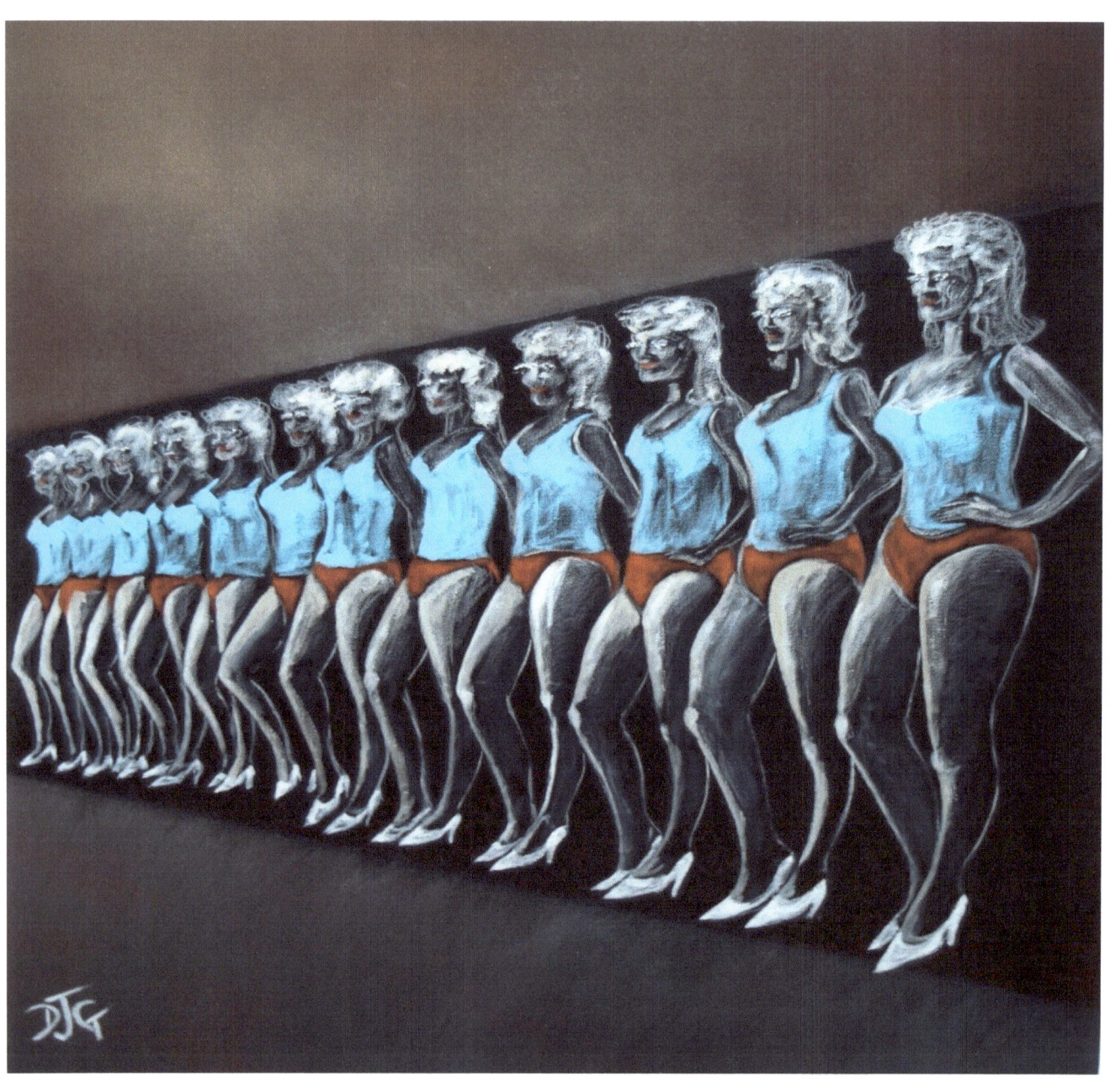

Chorus Line – Mixed Media on canvas – "24" x 30"

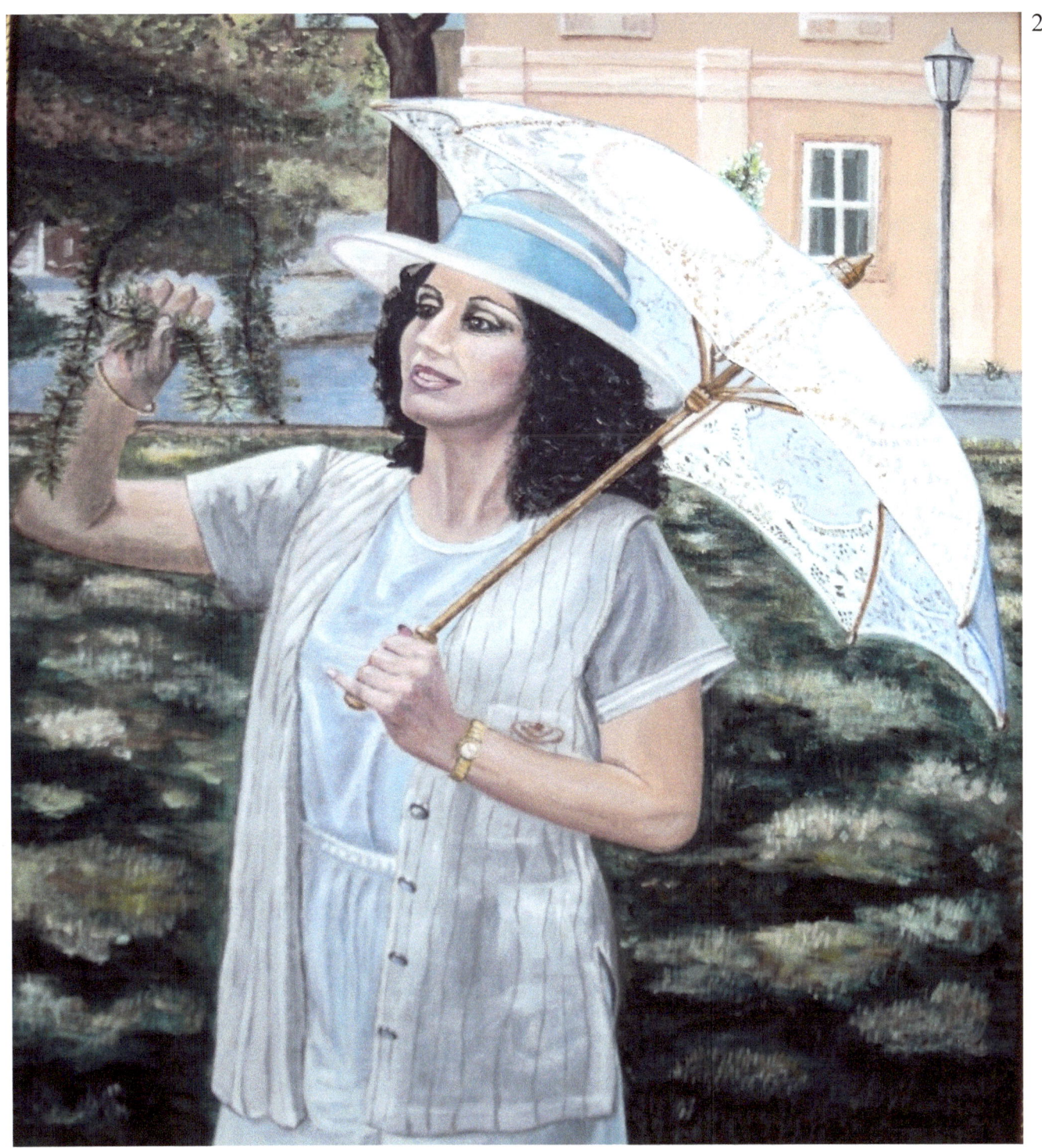

Savannah – Acrylic on canvas – 22" x 28"

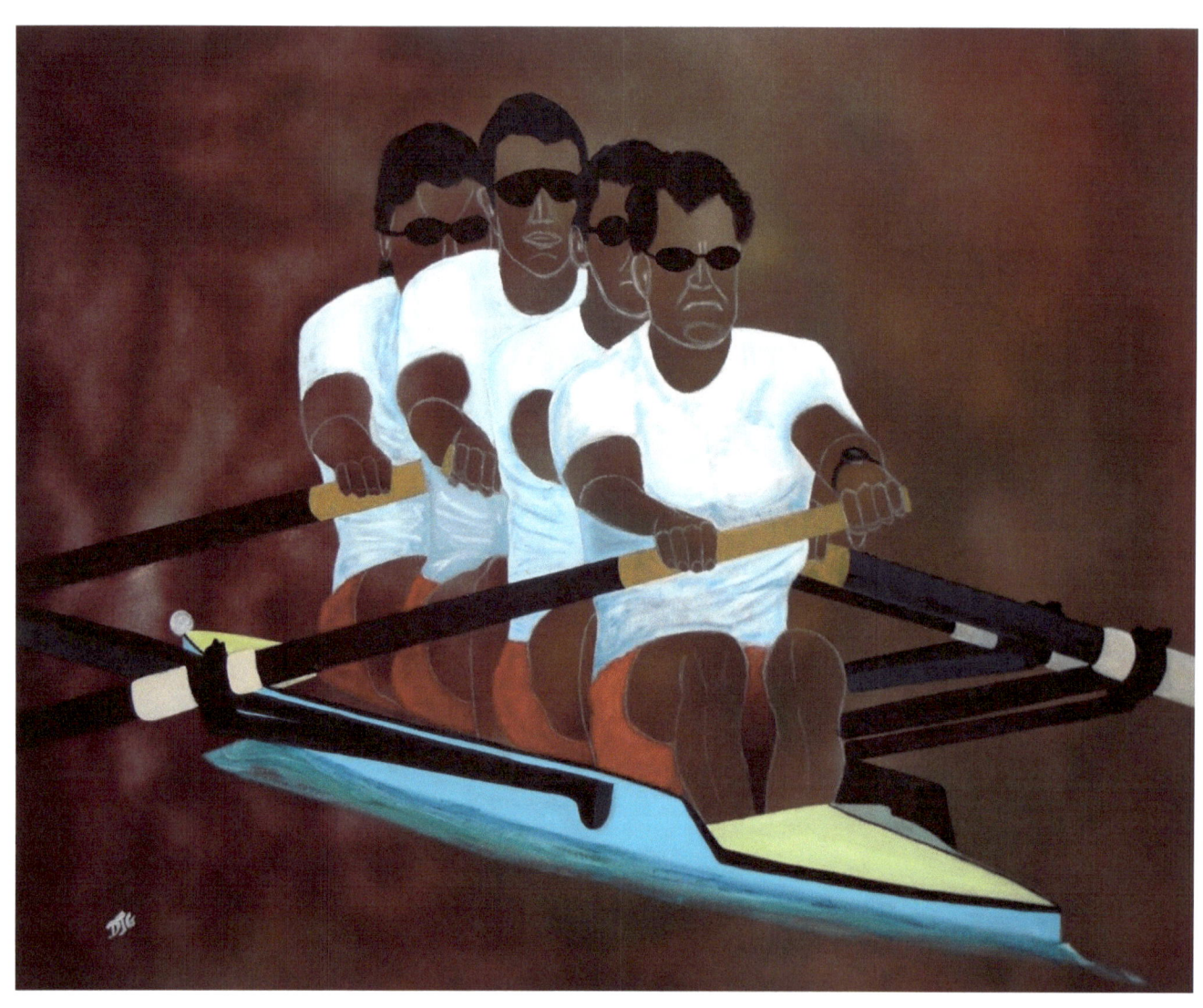

Coxless Four – Mixed Media on canvas – 30" x 40"

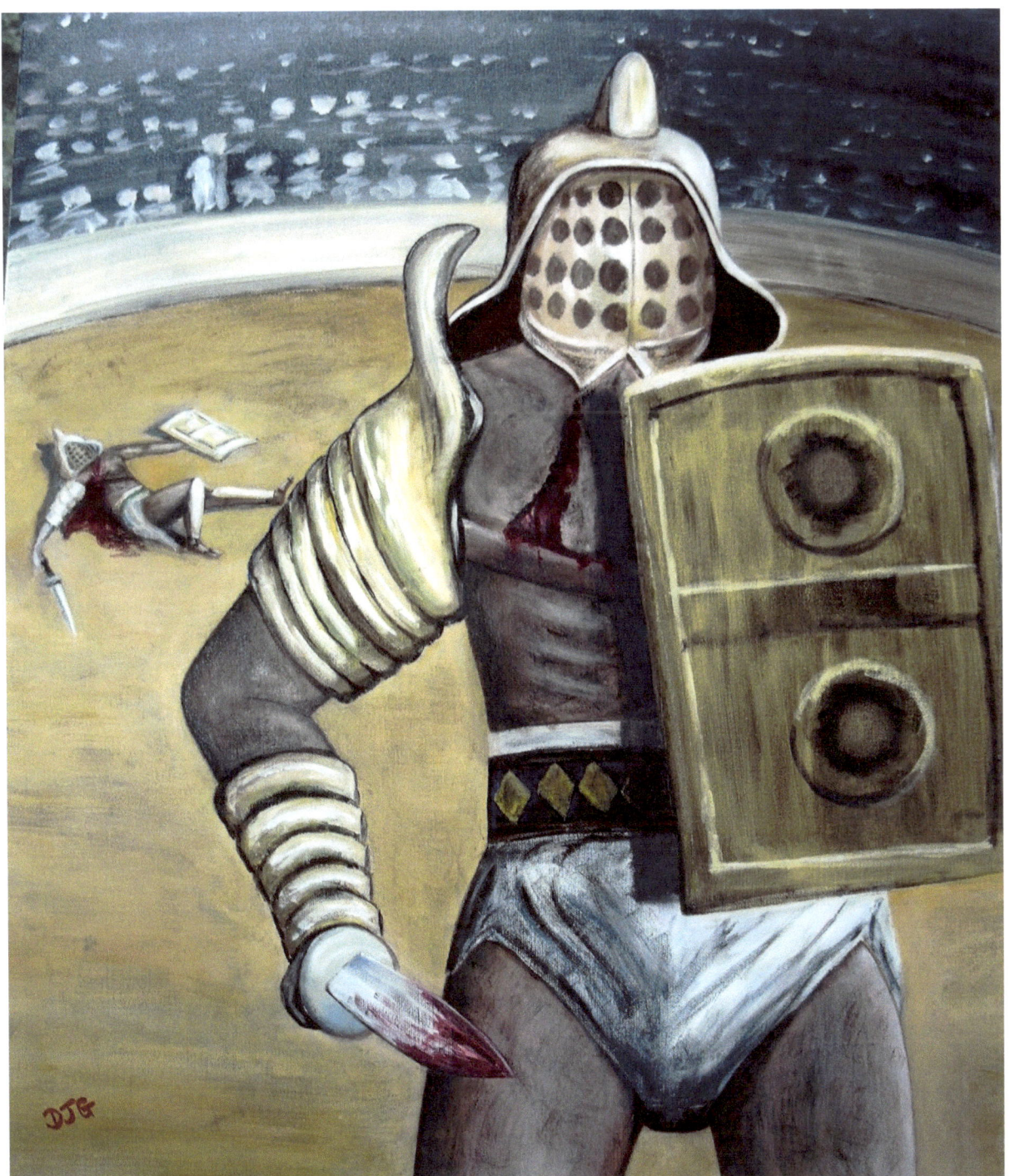

Gladiator – Acrylic on canvas -- 24" x 30"

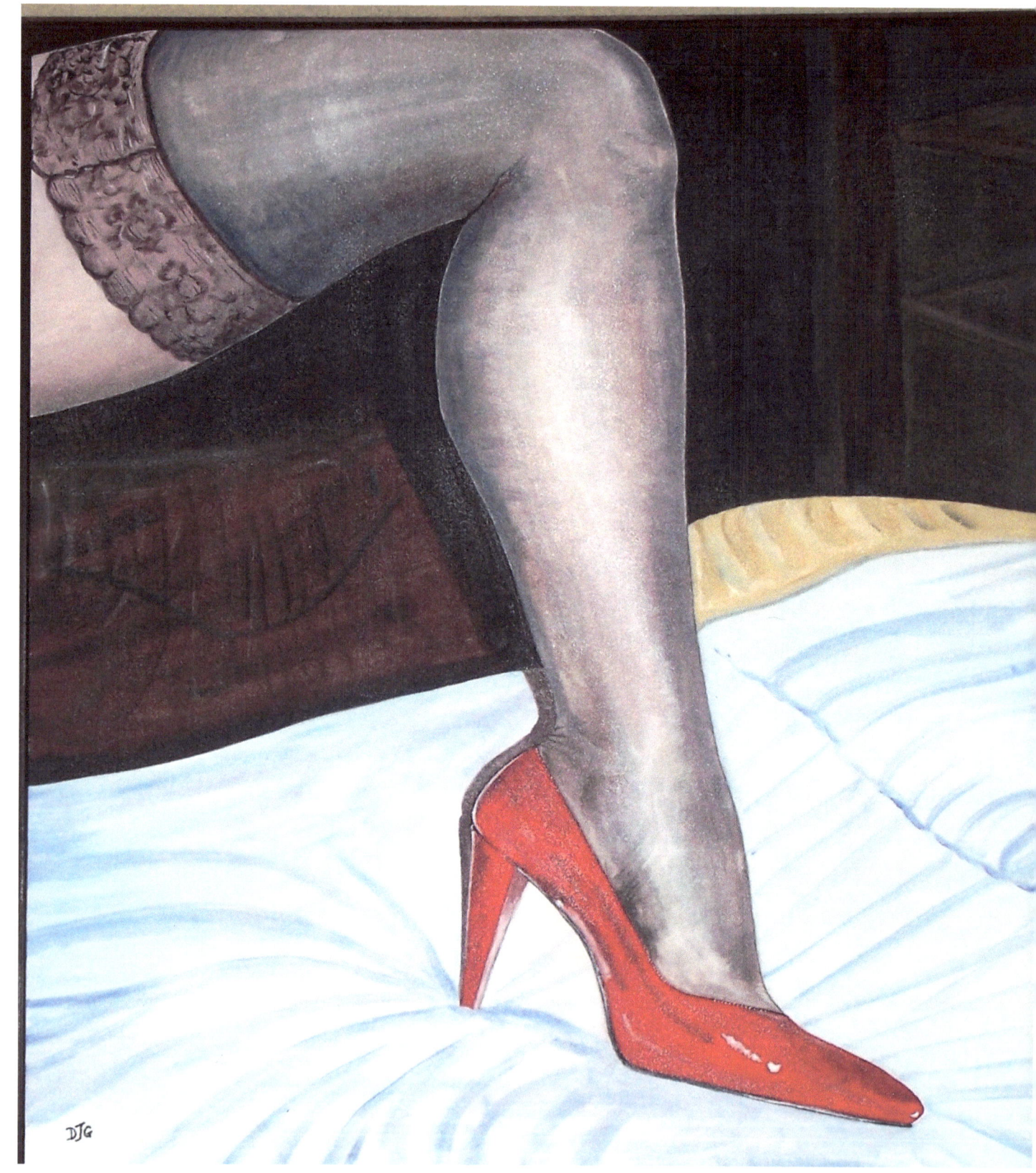

Red Shoe – Acrylic on Canvas -- 36" x 48"

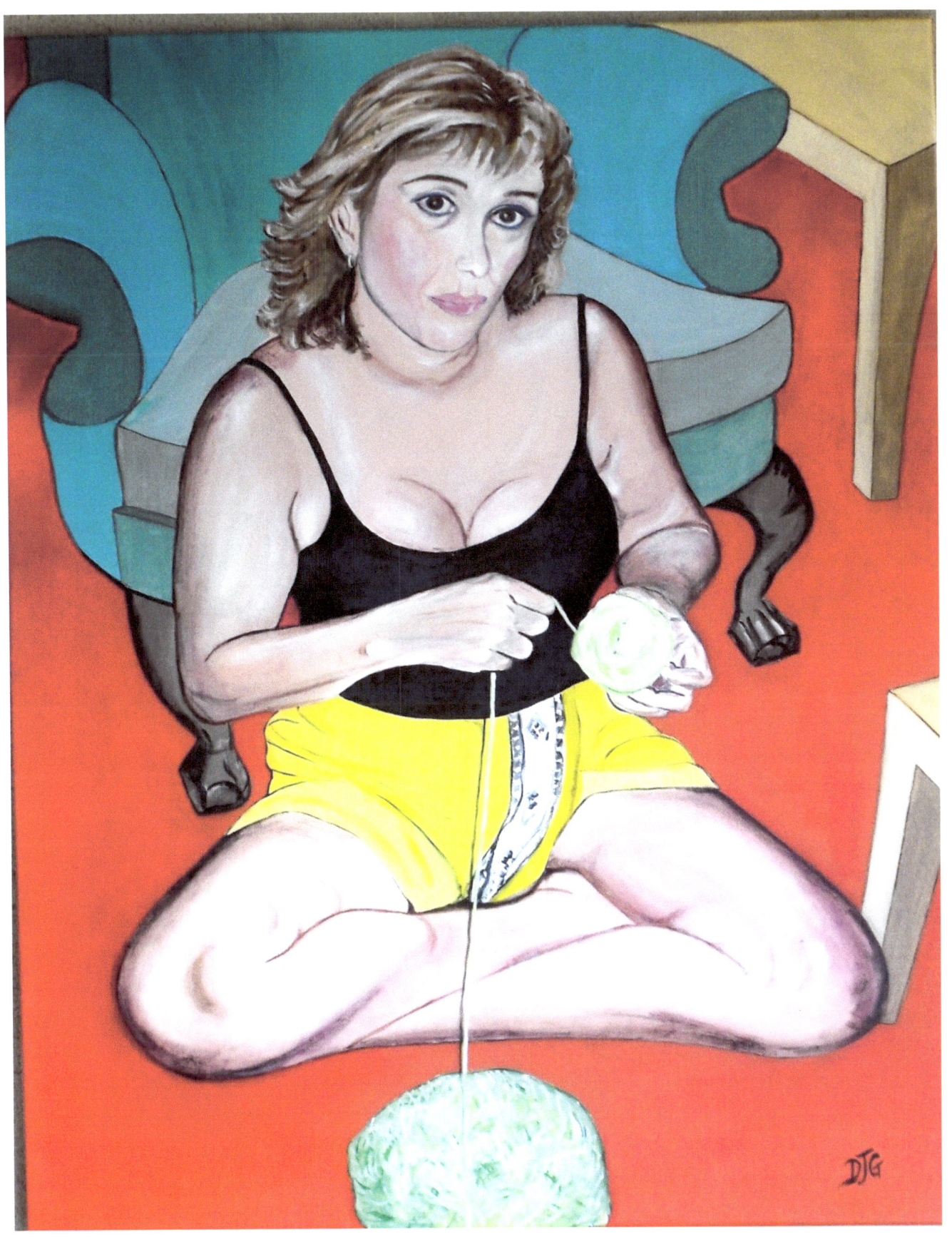

La Tricoteuse – Acrylic on canvas – 36" x 48"

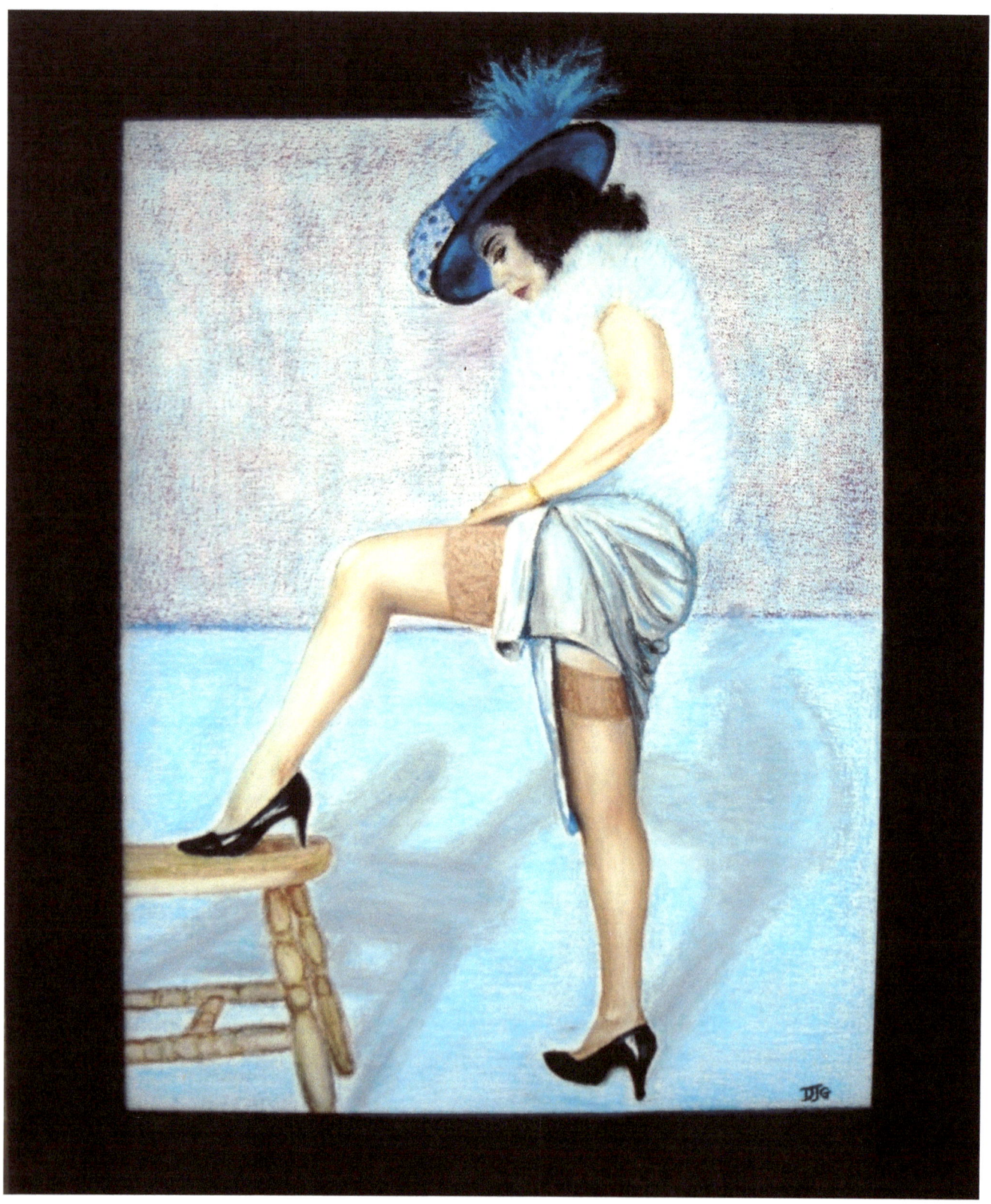

Adjusting Hose 1 -- Oil Pastel on canvas ---24" x 30"

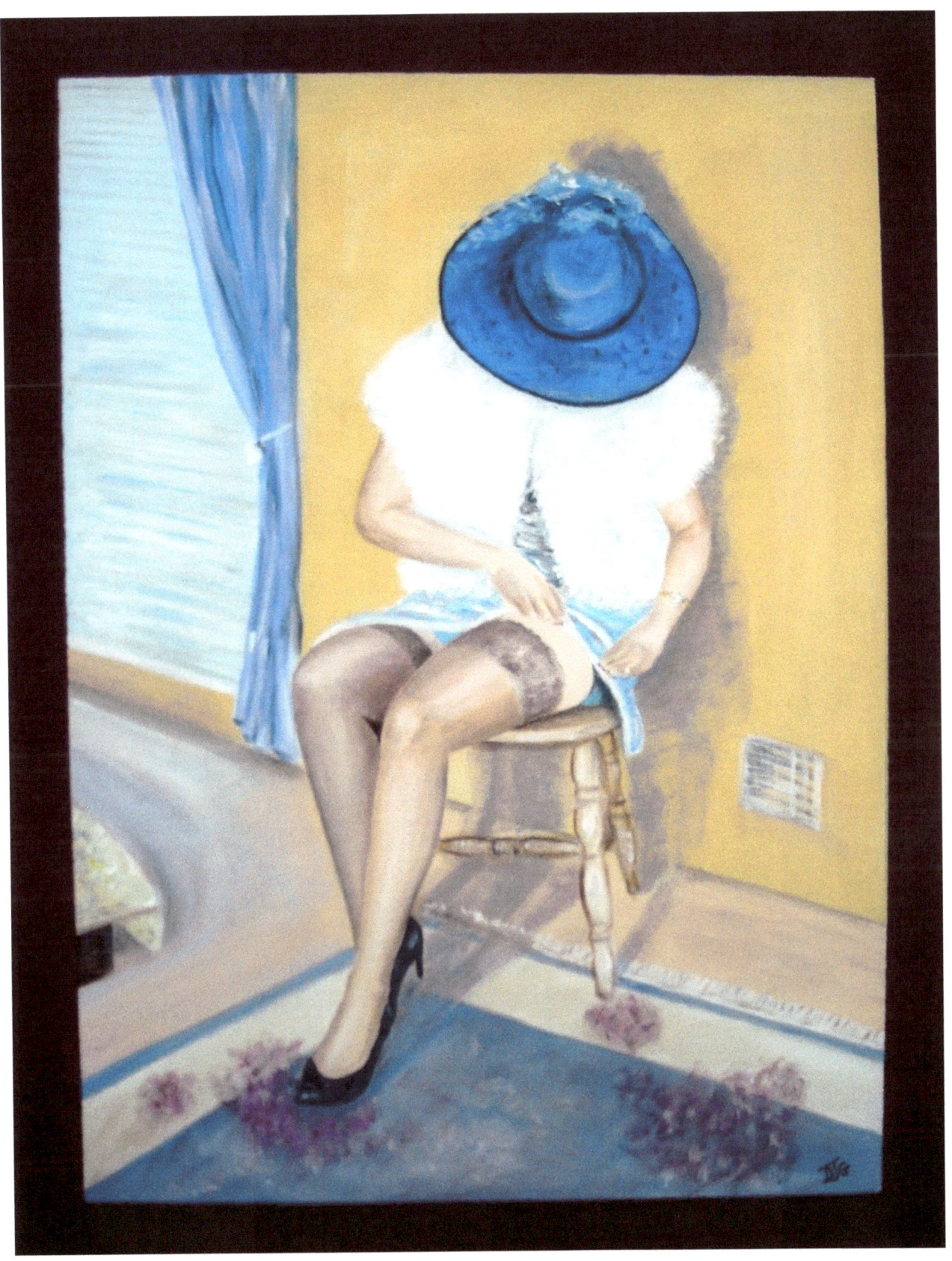

Adjusting Hose 2 – Acrylic on canvas – 18" x 24"

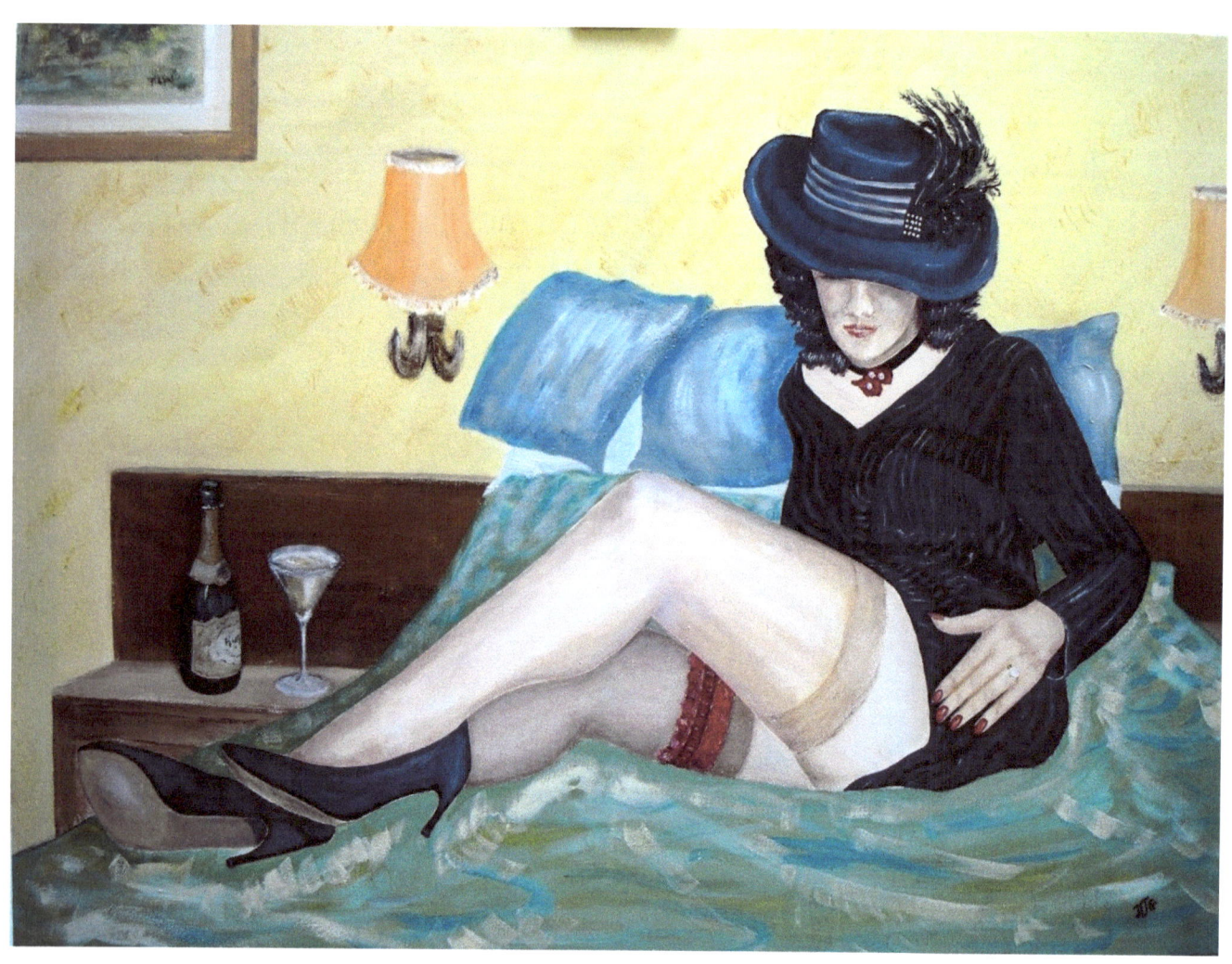

After a Hard Day – Acrylic on canvas – 24" x 36"

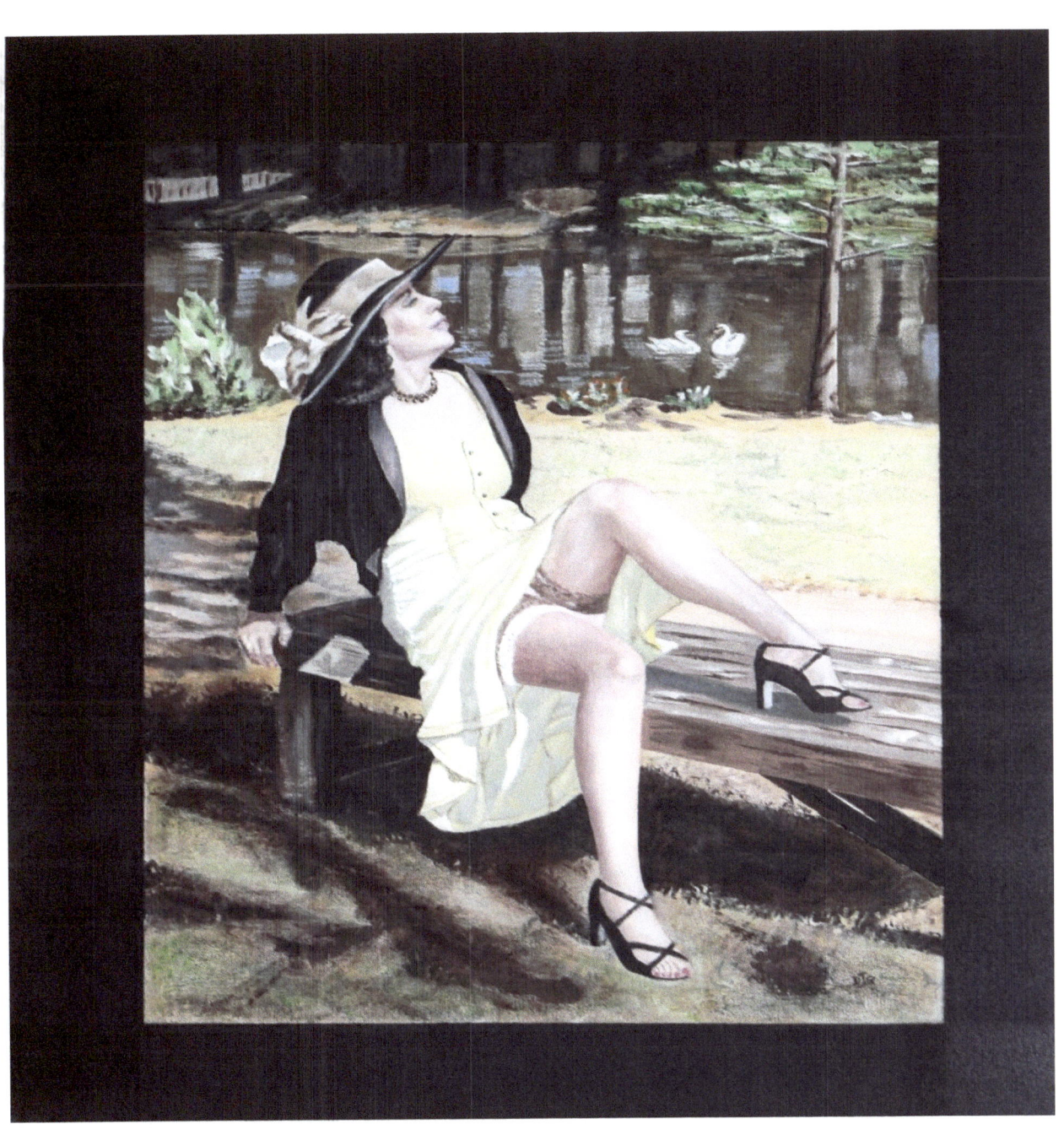

Sunning in the Park – Acrylic on canvas – 22" x 28"

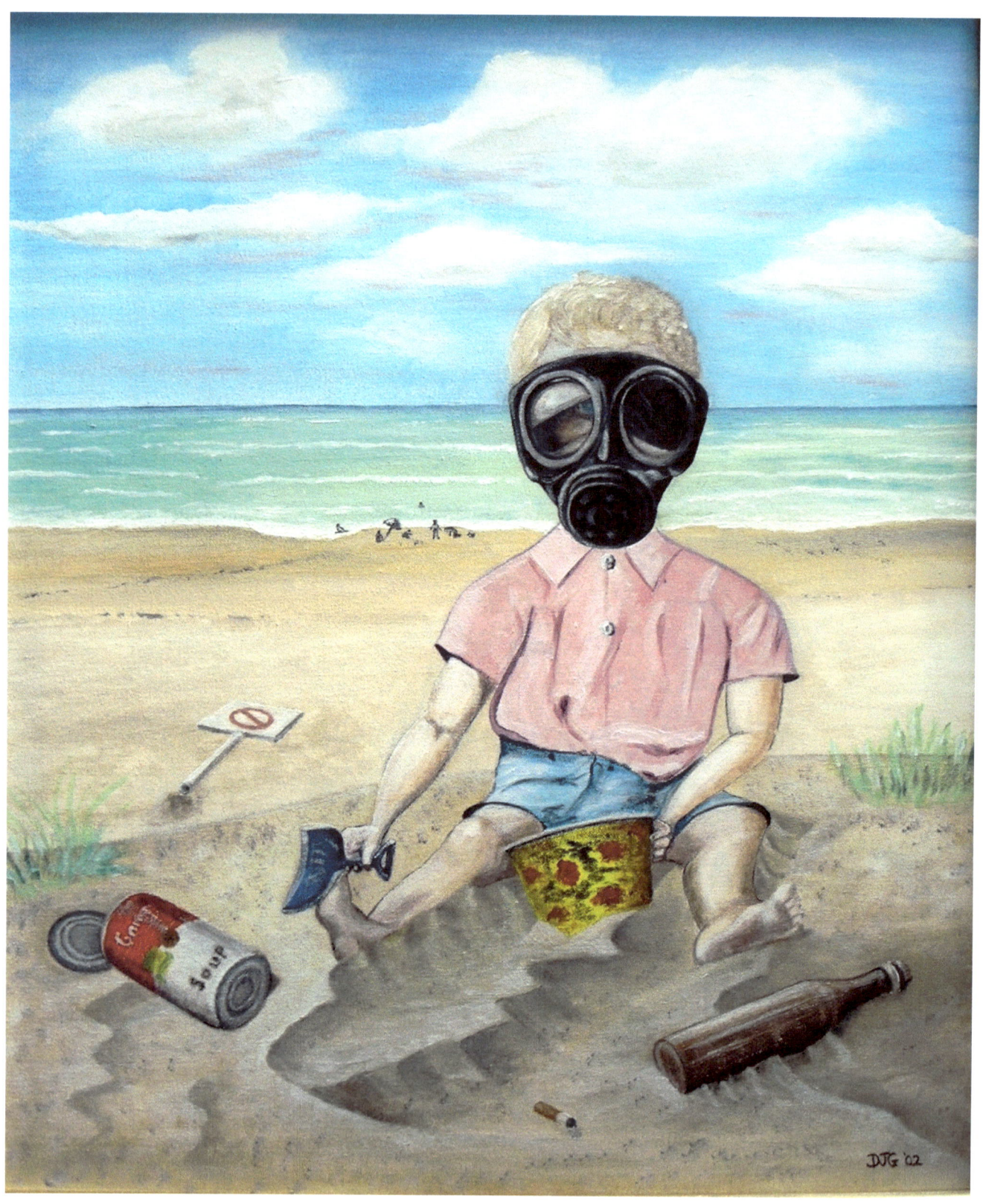

My Legacy, My Garden – Acrylic on canvas -- 24" x 30"

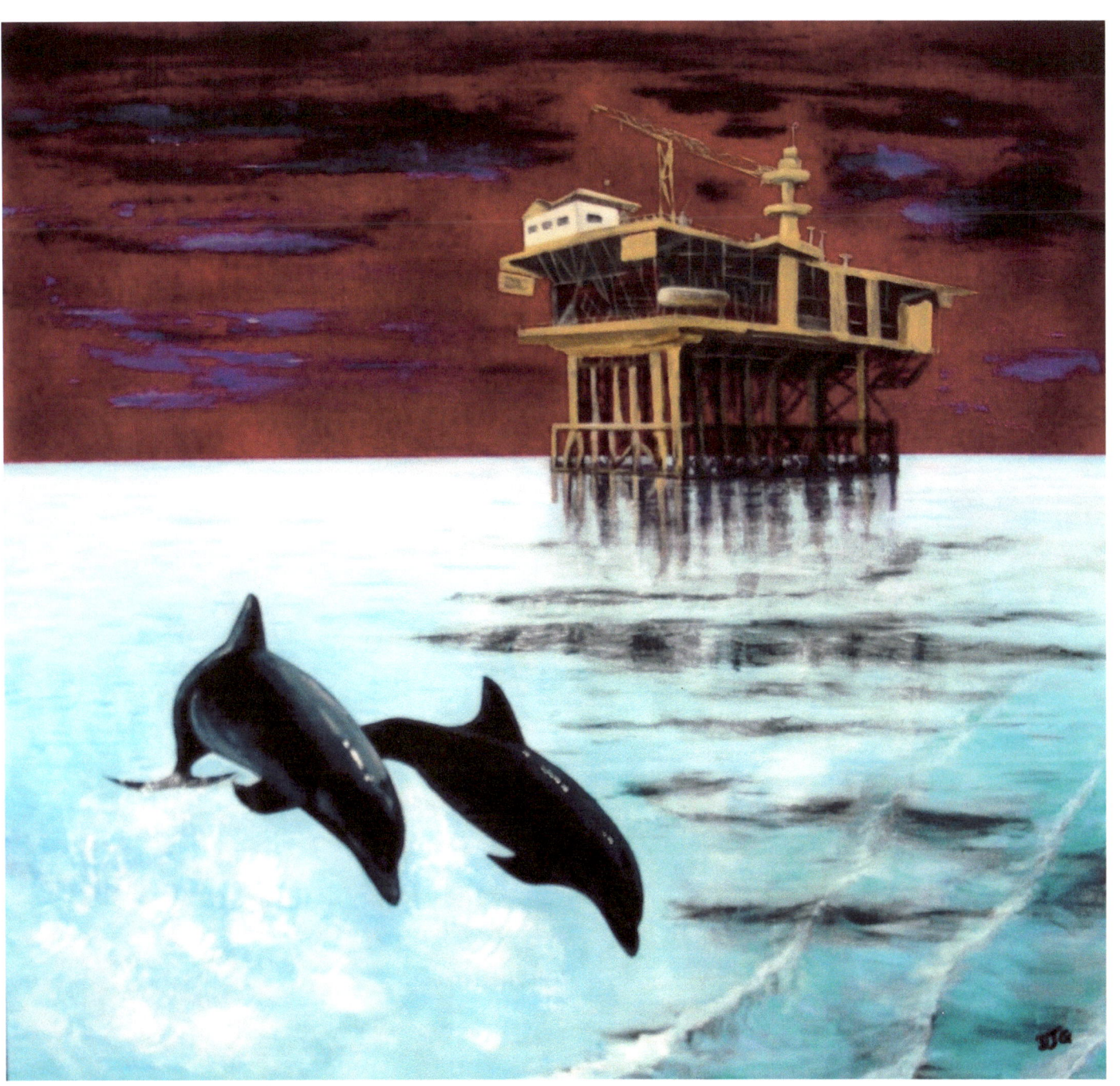

Pollution By Sea (2 of 3) – Acrylic on canvas –36" x 36"

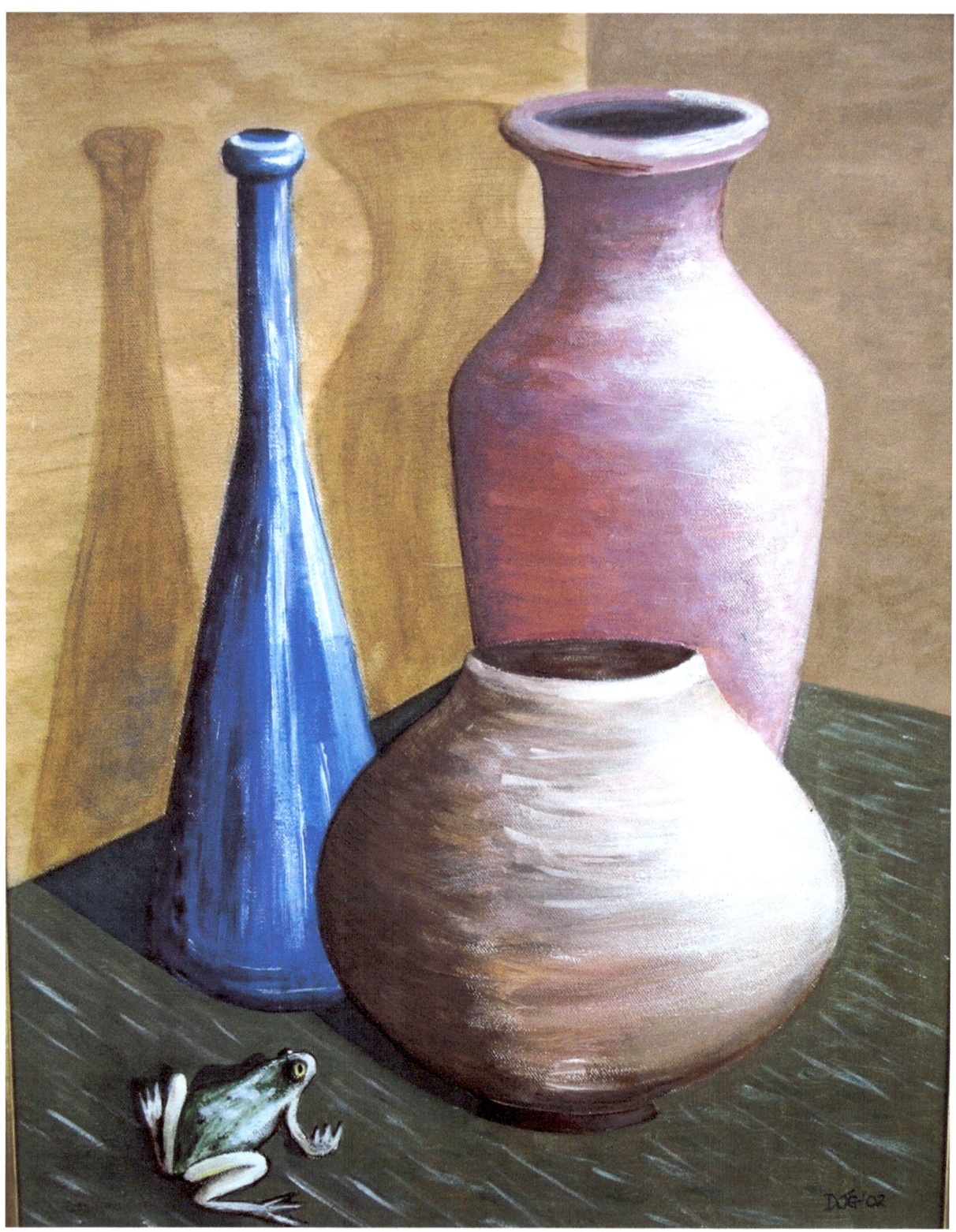

Pots, Bottle and Frog -- Acrylic on canvas – 16" x 20"

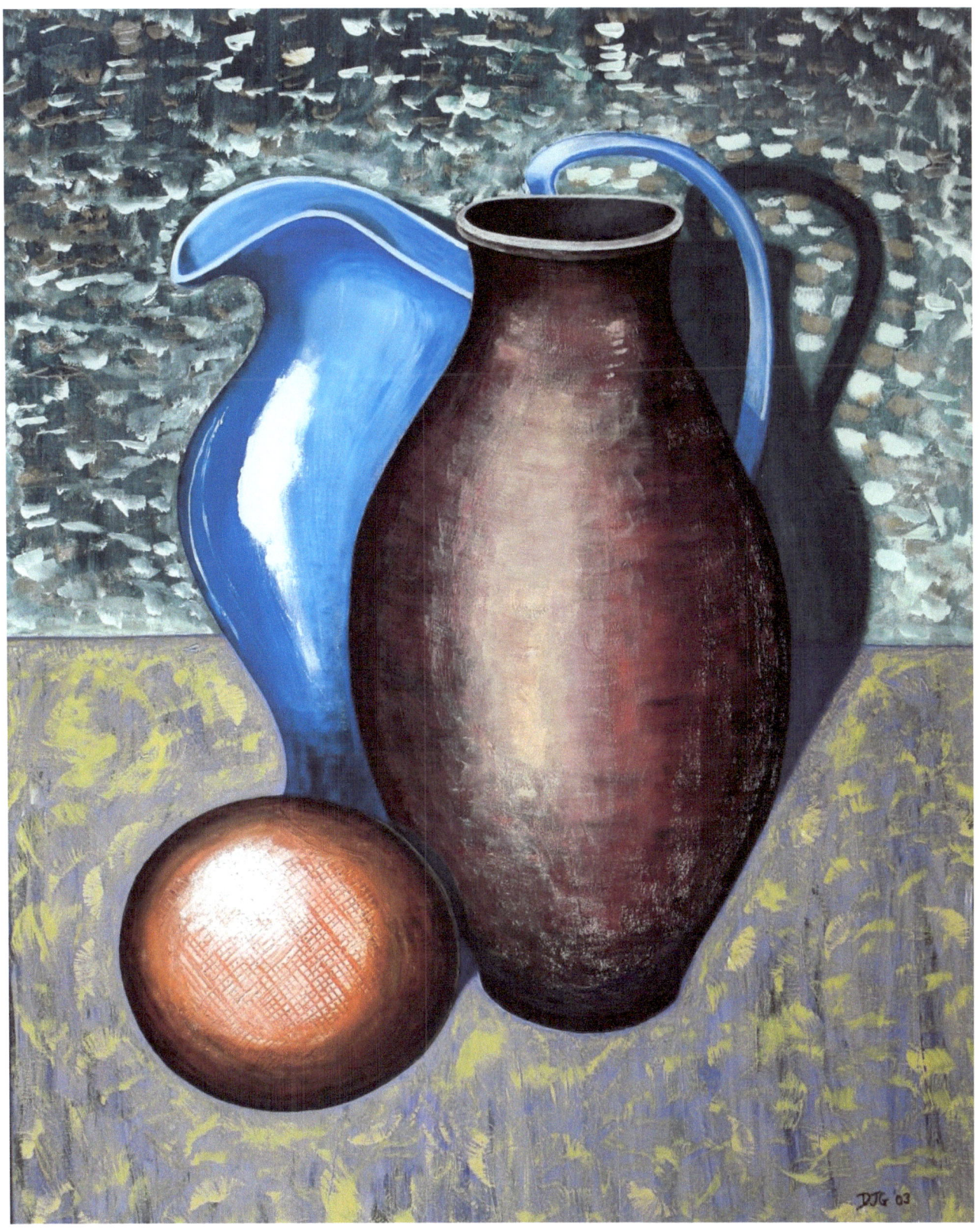

Jug, Pot, and Ball – Acrylic on canvas – 36" x 48"

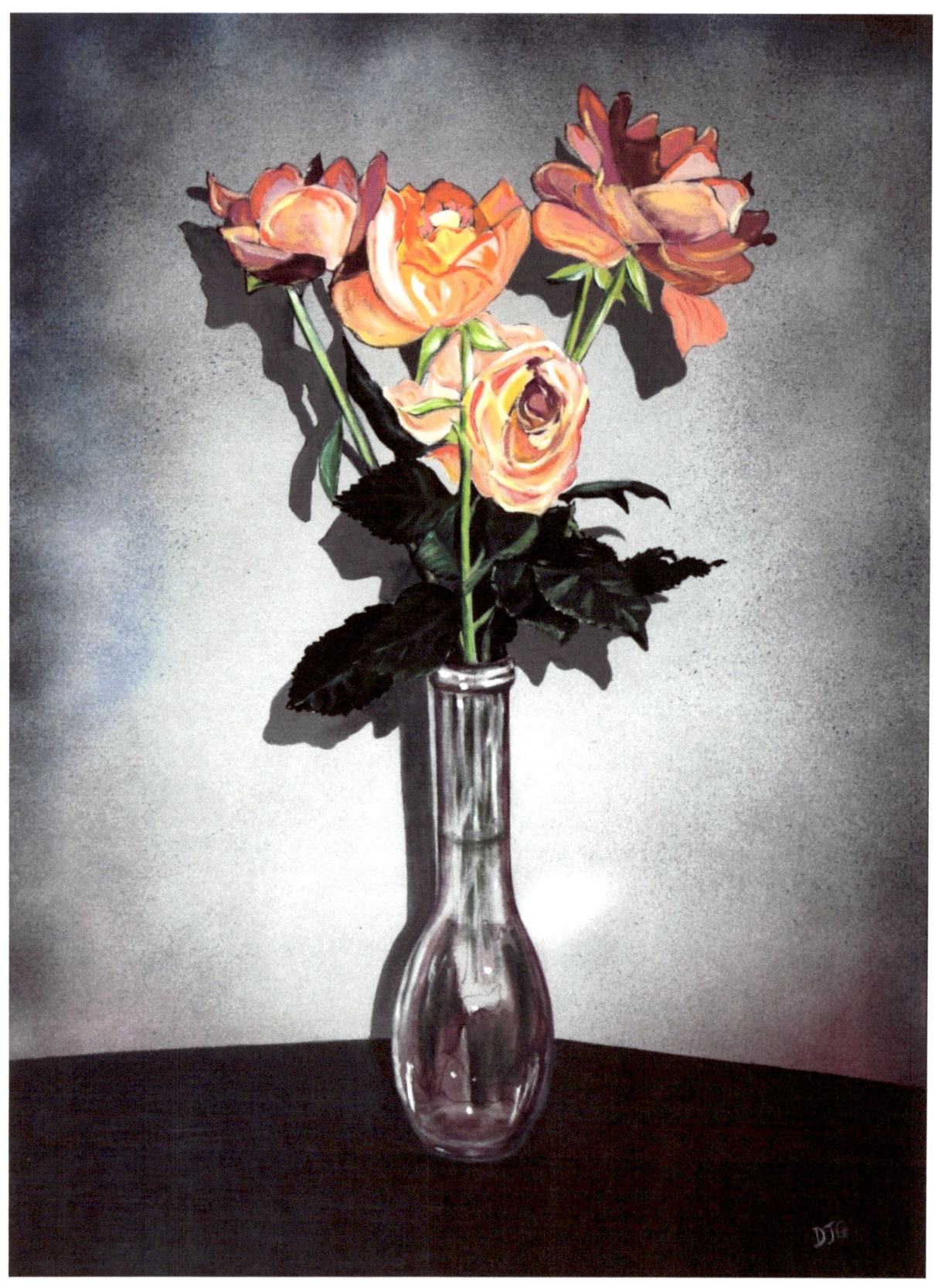

Roses 2 -- Acrylic on canvas - 30" x 40"

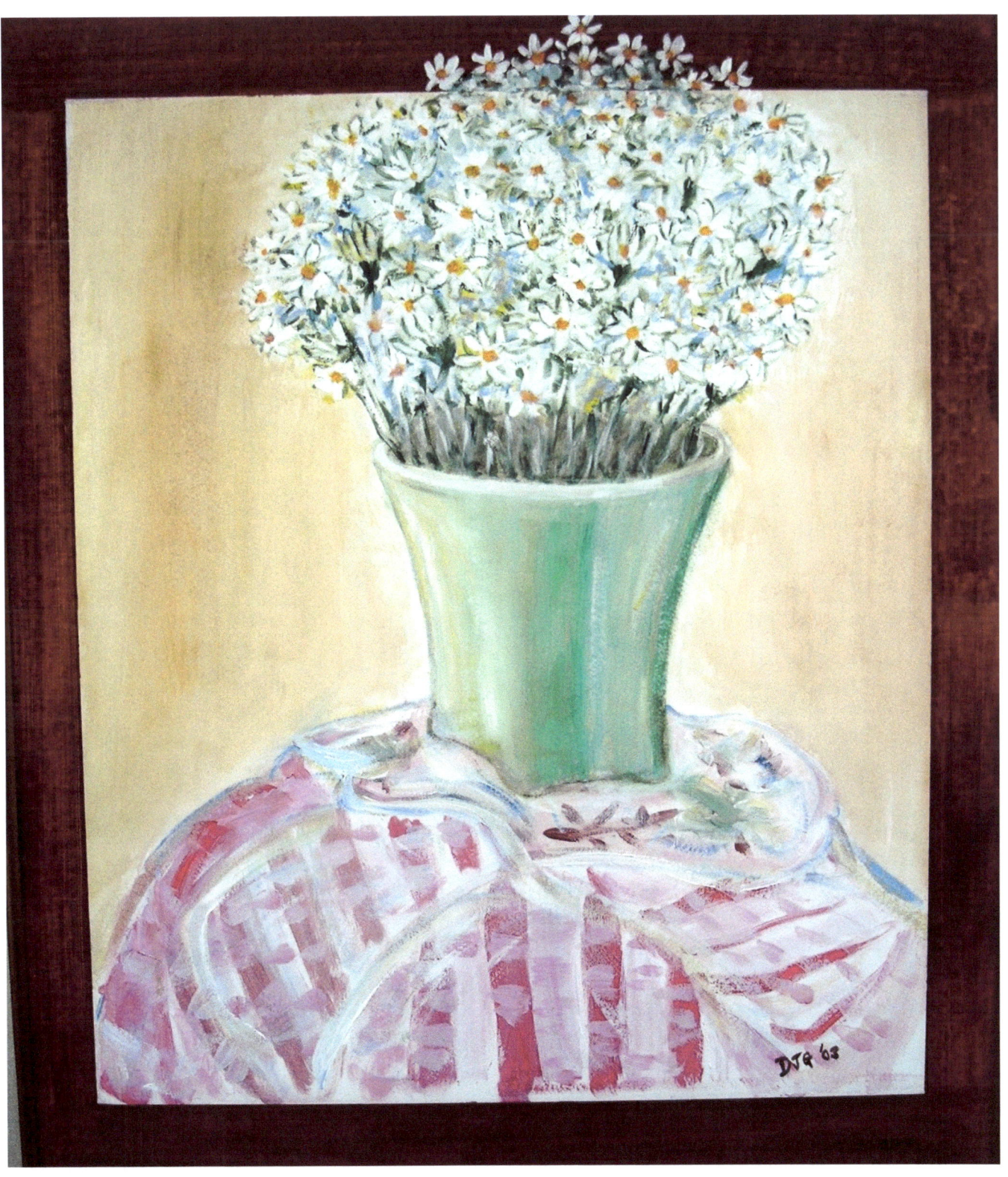

Daises – Acrylic on board – 18" x 24"

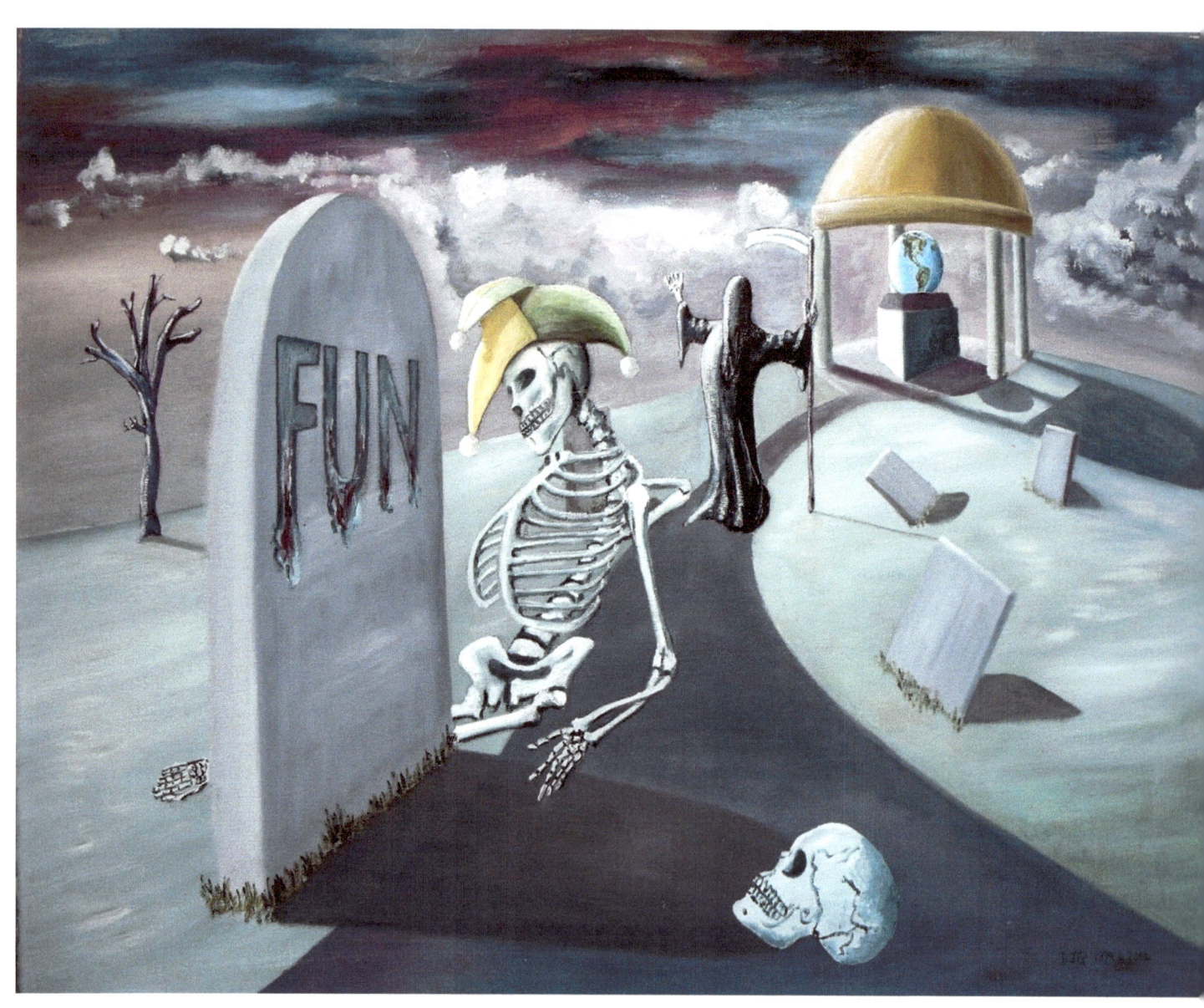

Death Of Fun – oil on canvas - 20" x 30"

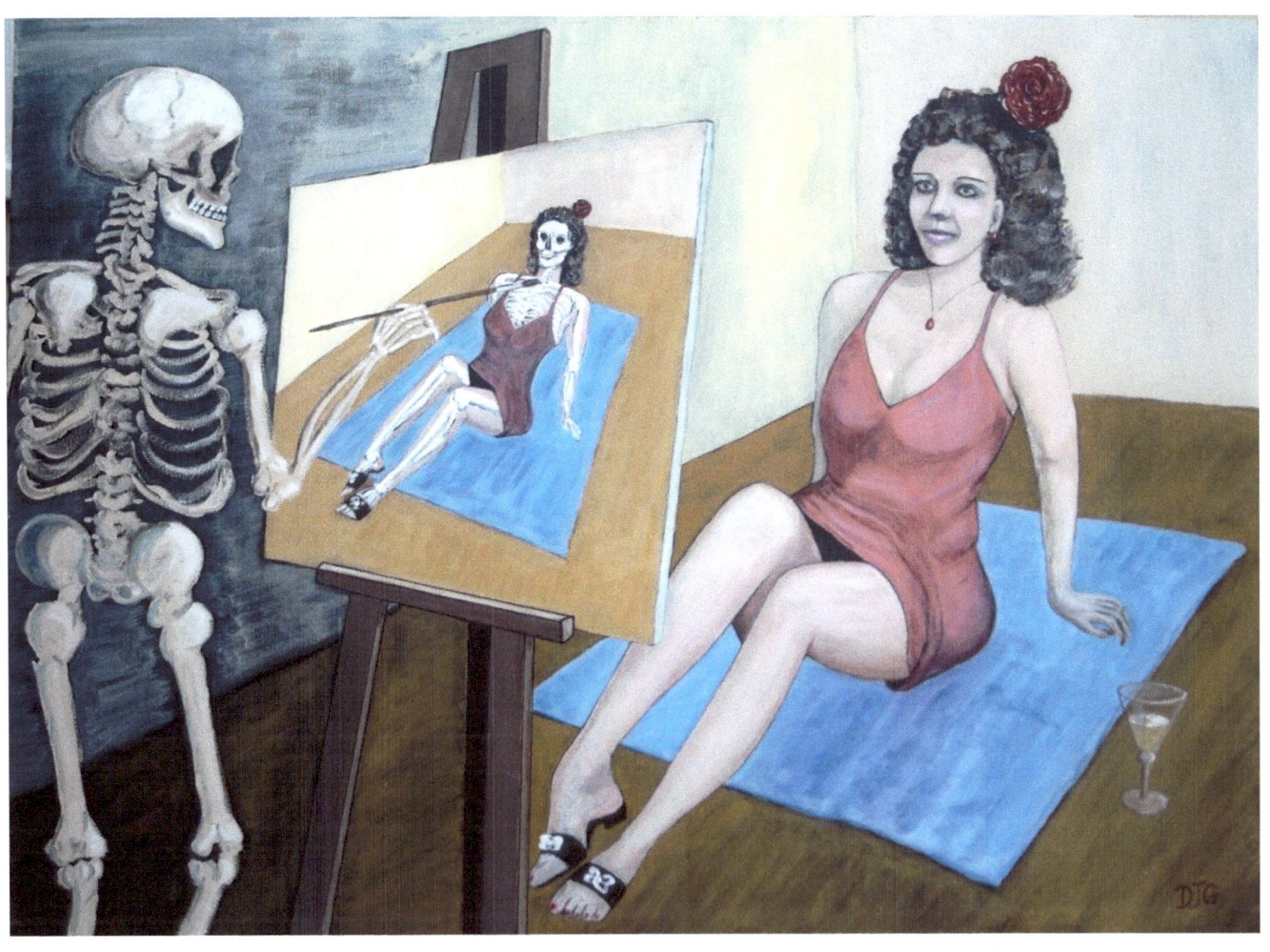

In the Eye of the Beholder – Acrylic on canvas – 36" x 48"

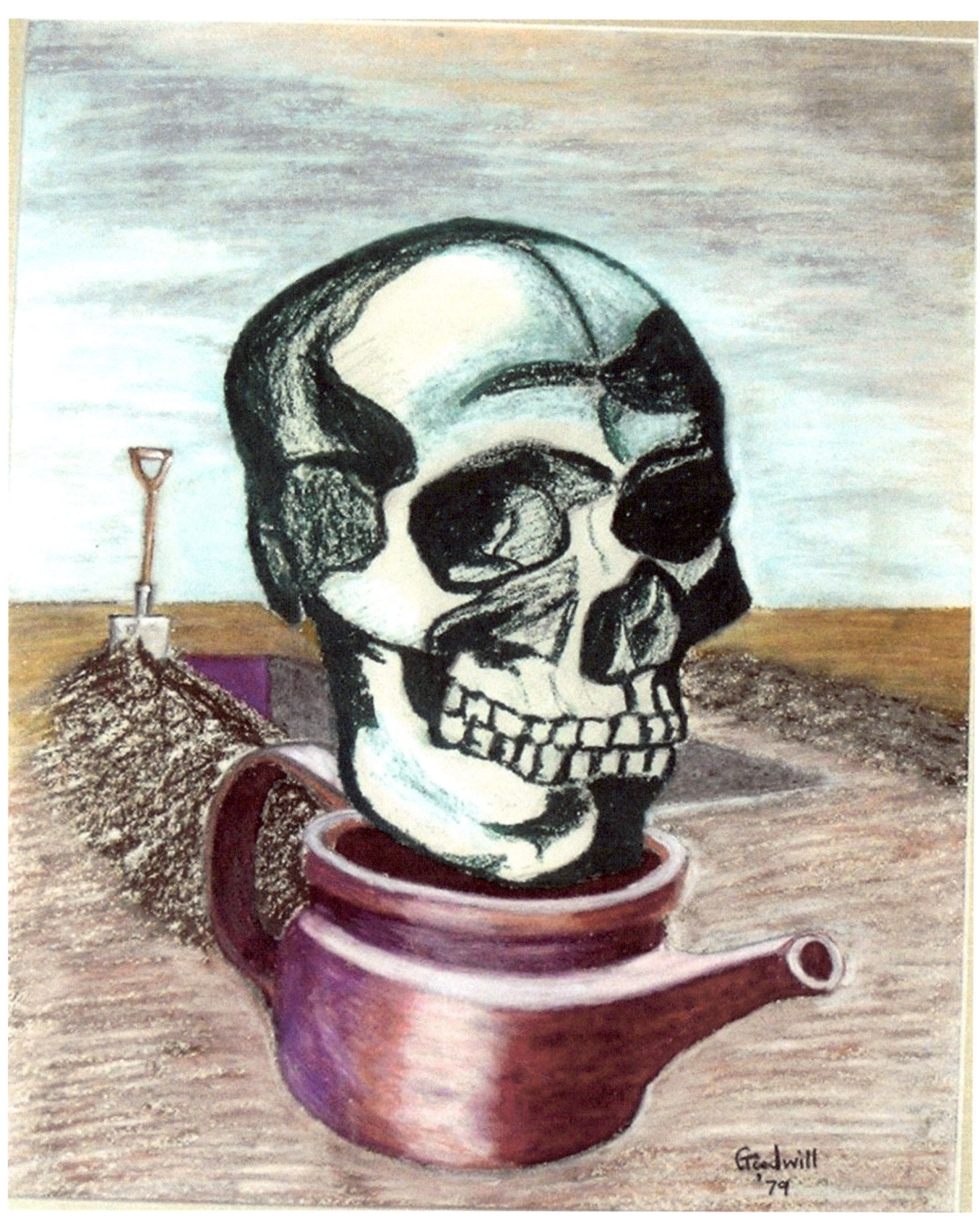

Let's Make Tea – Oil Pastel on paper – 12" x 16"

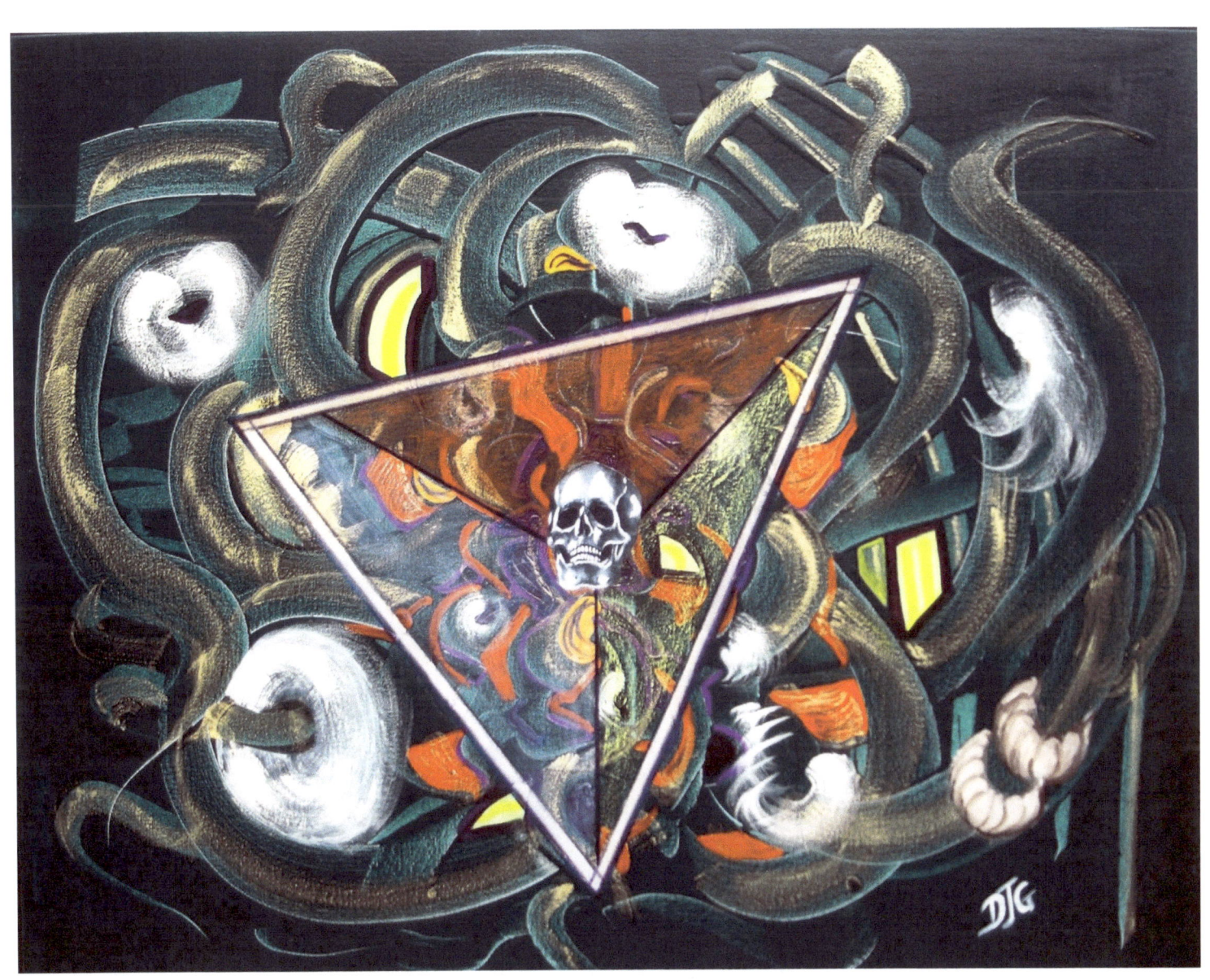

Phantasm – Mixed media on canvas – 36" x 48"

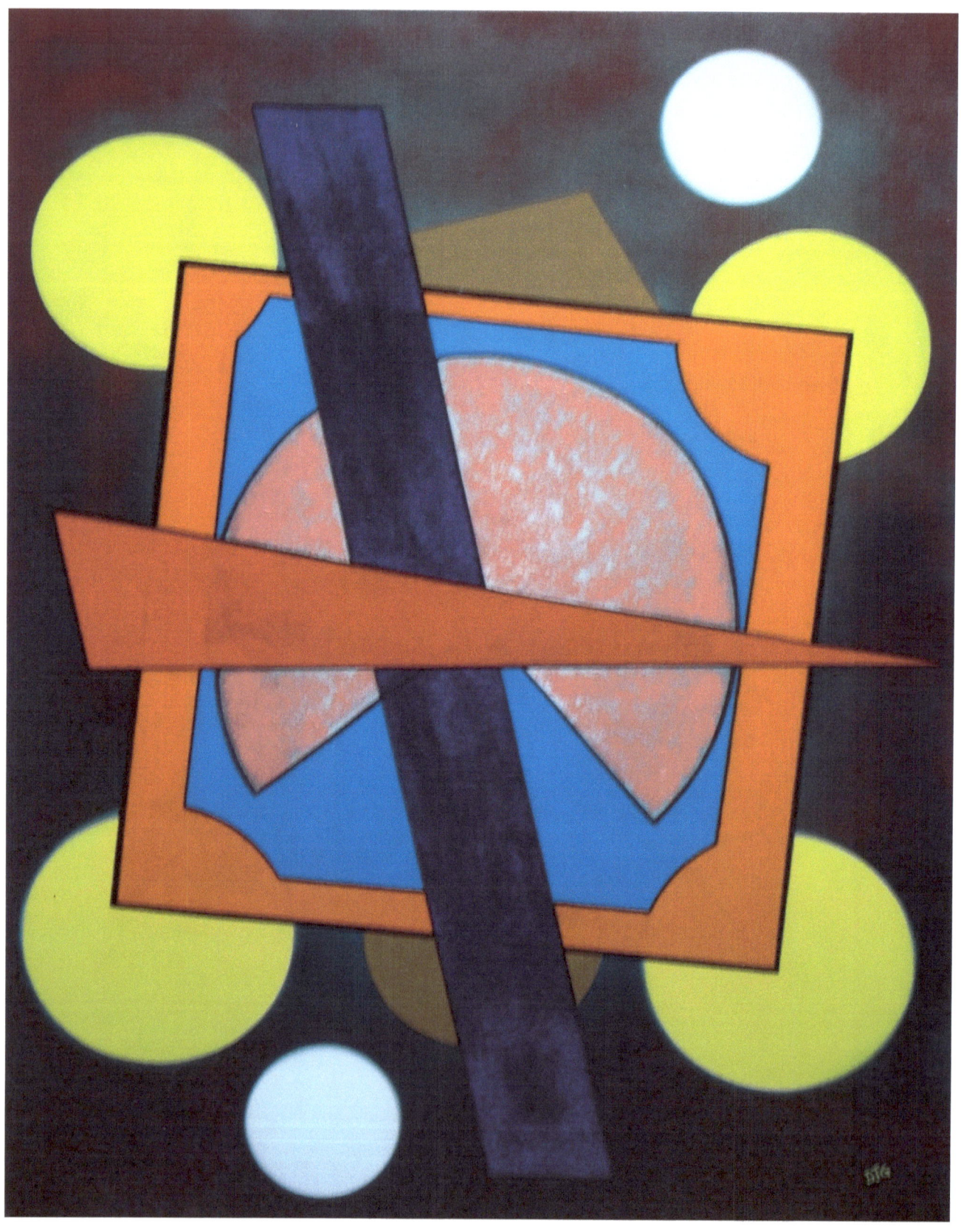

To The Point – Acrylic on canvas – 36" x 48"

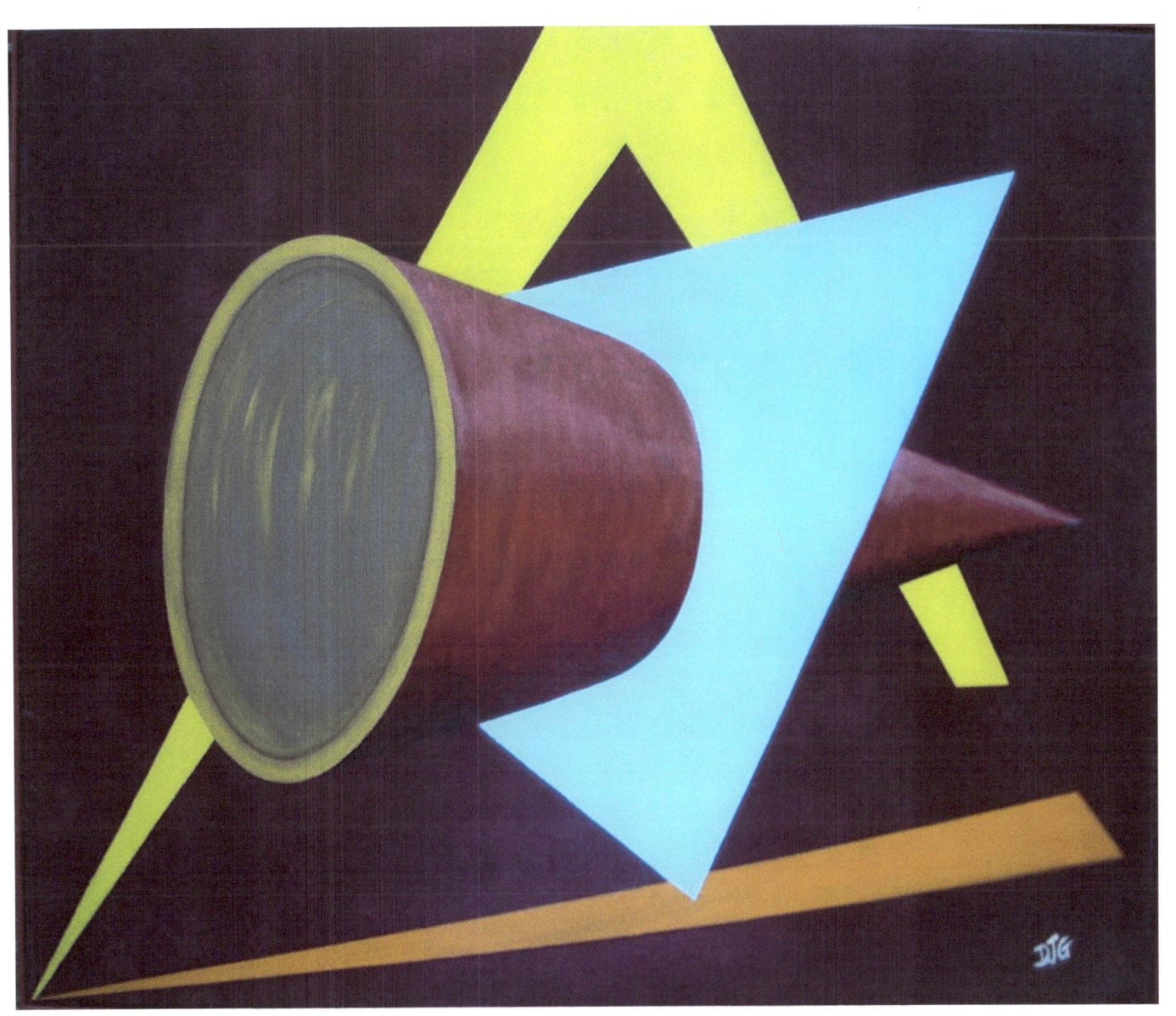

Penetration – Acrylic on canvas – 36" x 48"

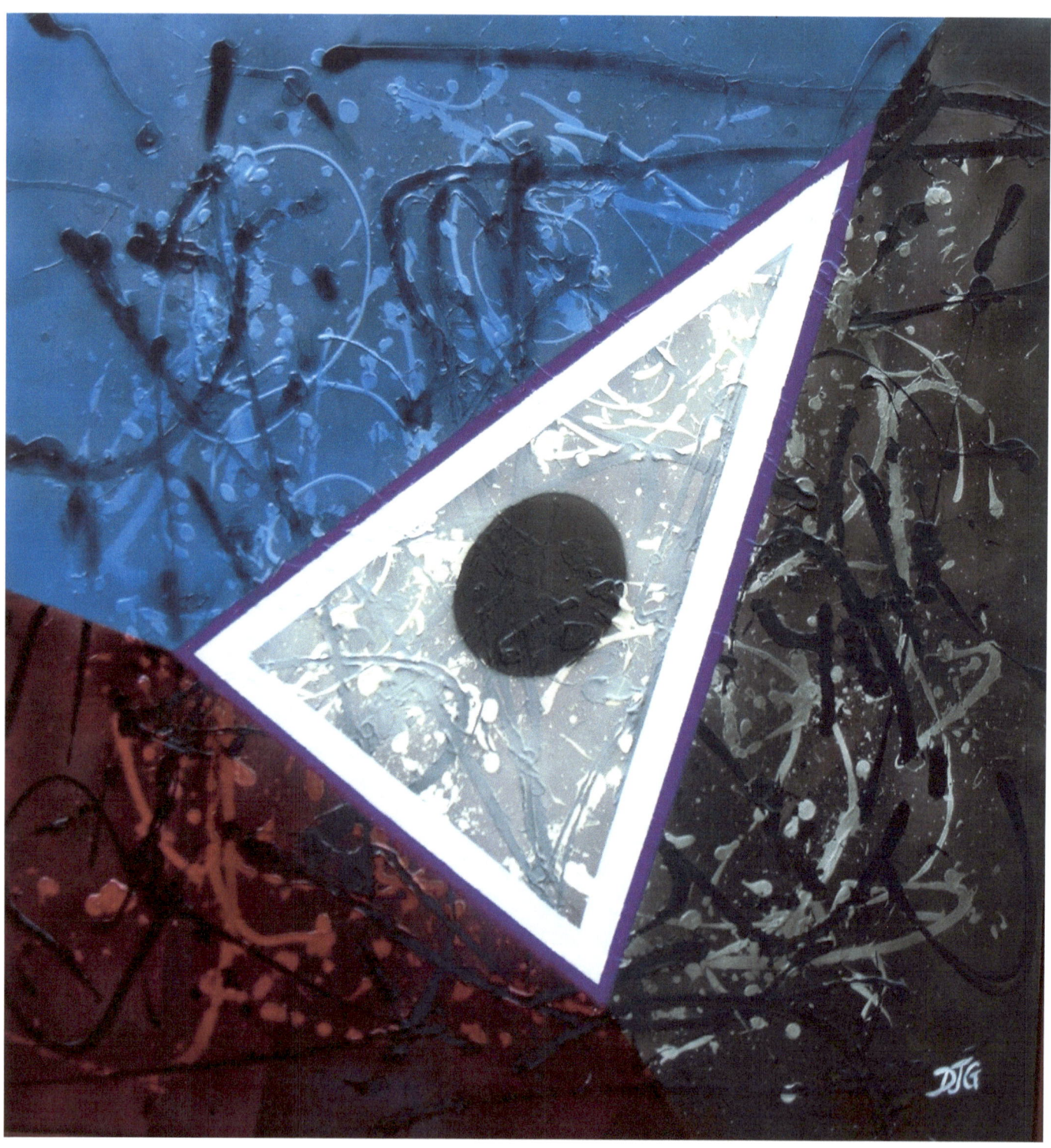

Isosceles – Acrylic on canvas – 48" x 48"

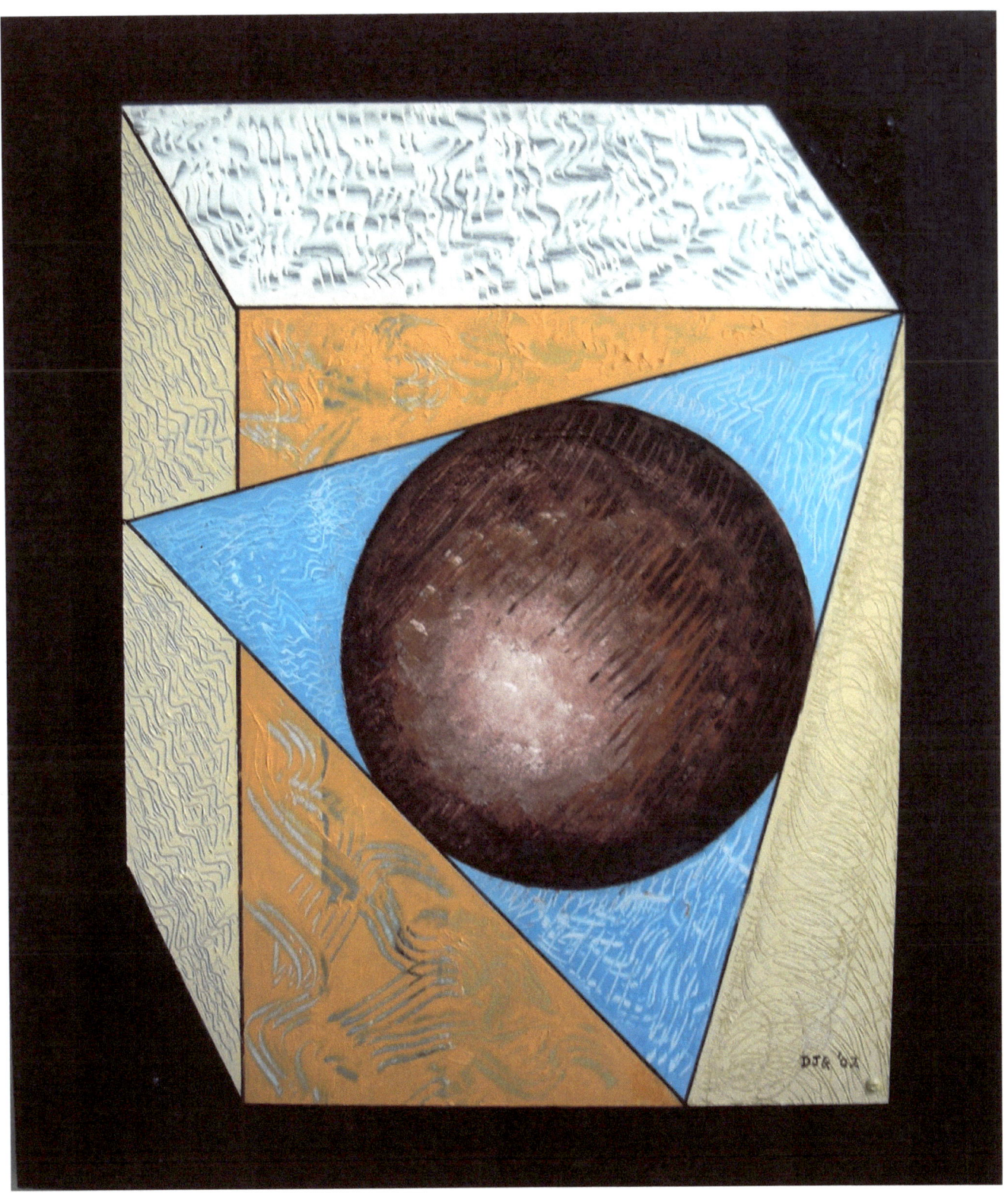

Equilateral – Acrylic on board -- 16" x 20"

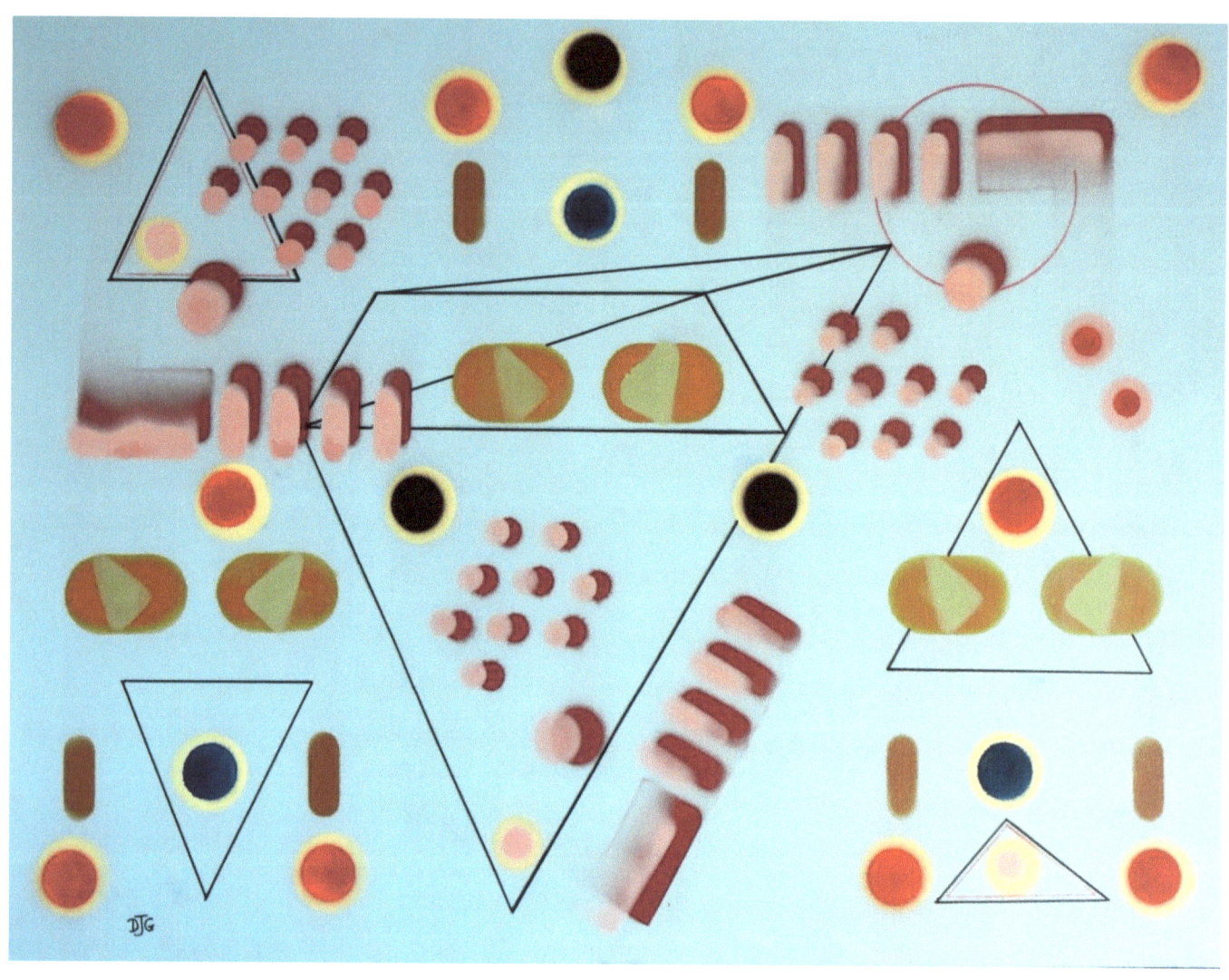

Triangles and Dots – Mixed media – 36" x 48"

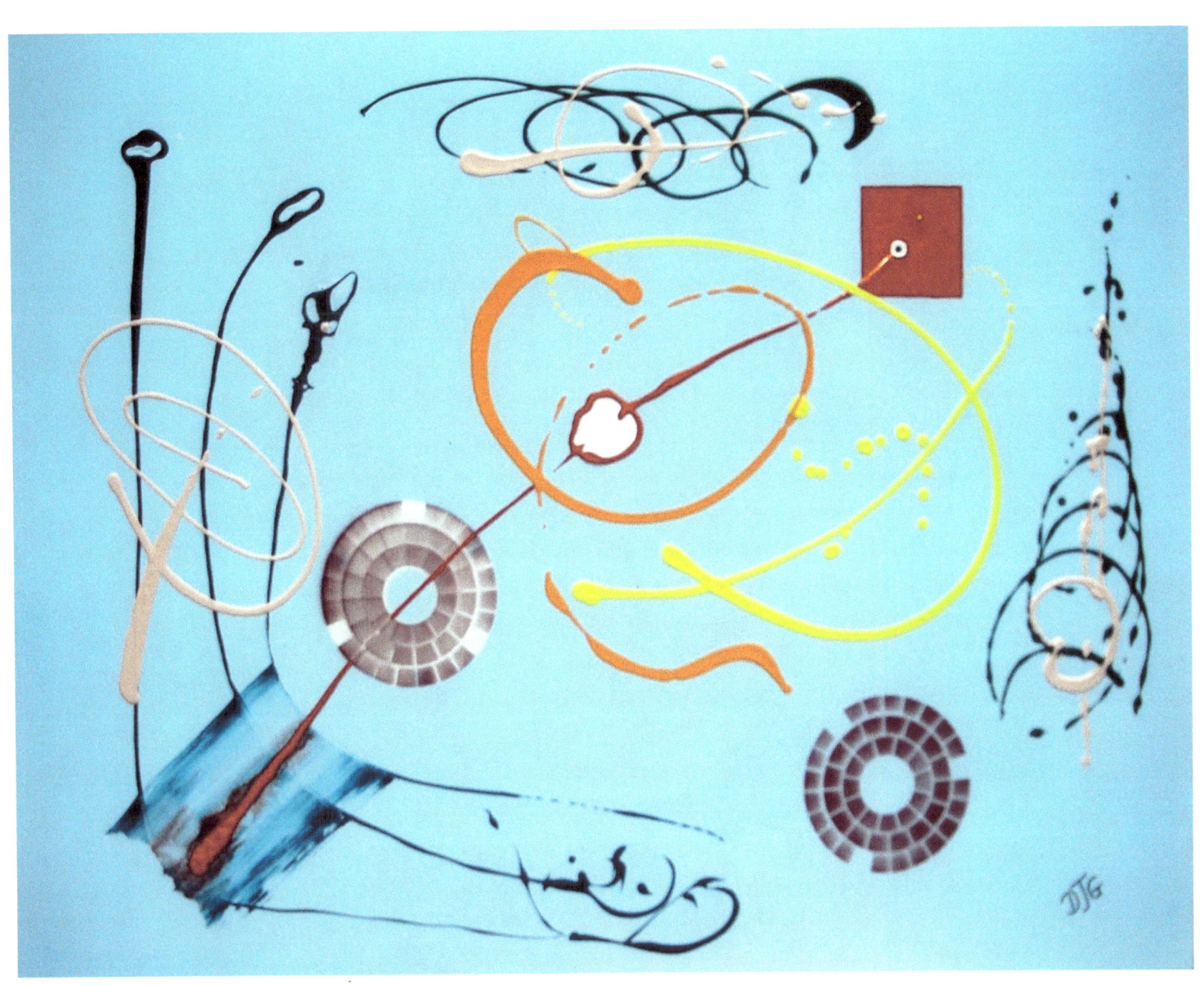

Organisms – Acrylic on canvas – 30" x 40"

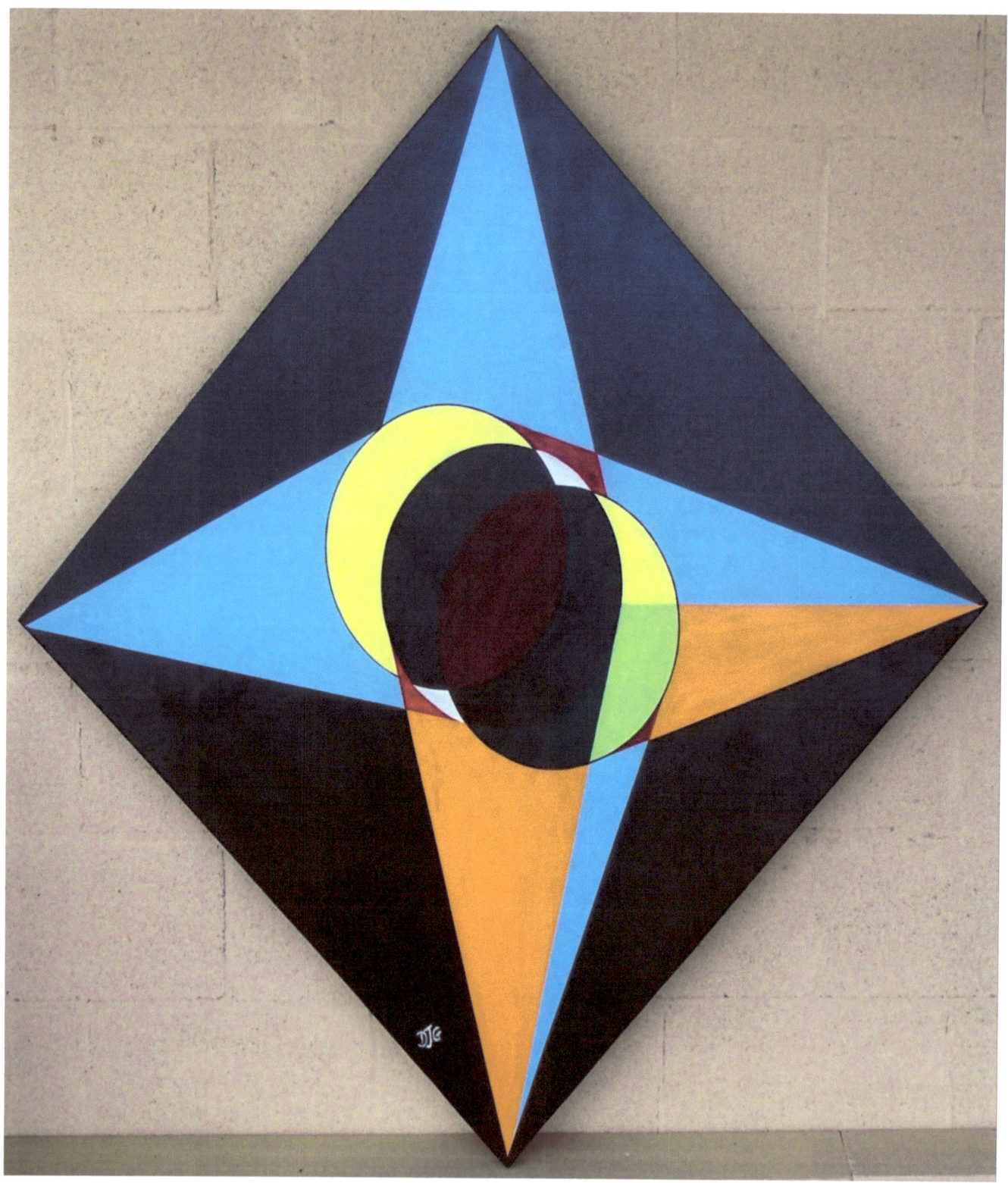

Illusion – Acrylic on canvas – 36" x 36"

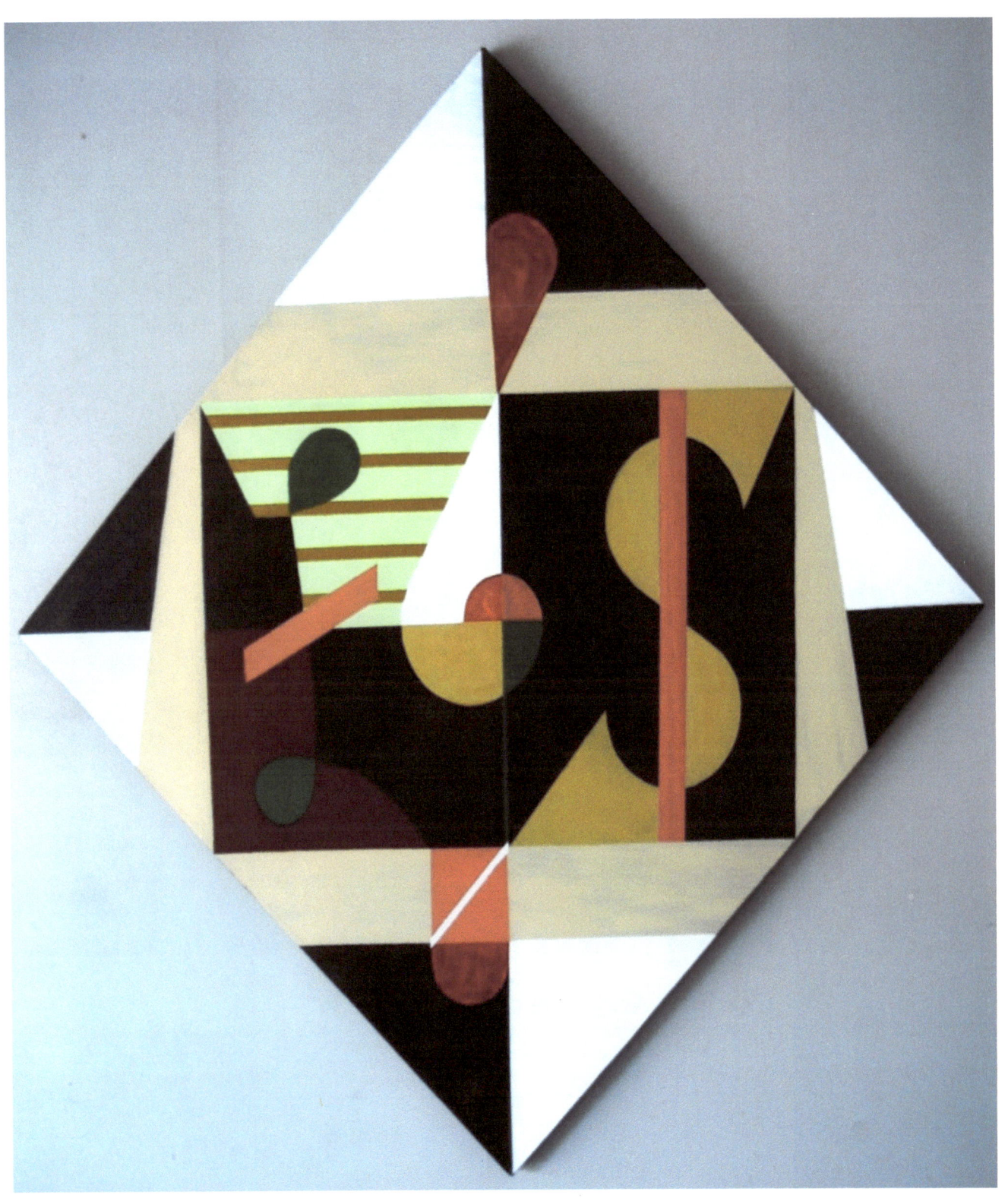

There's Money in Music – Acrylic on canvas – 36" x 36 "

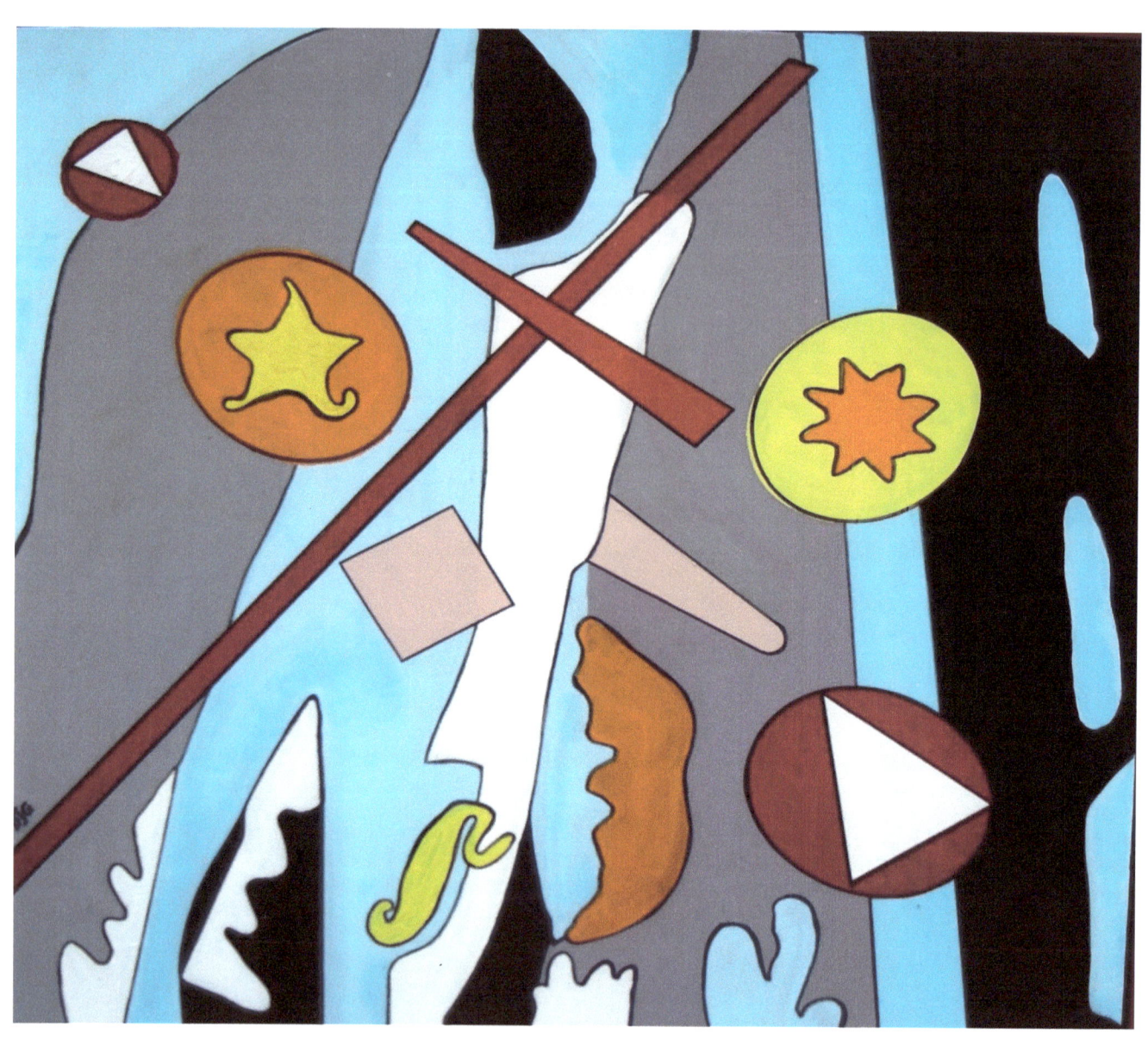

Crucifix – Acrylic on canvas – 36" x 36"

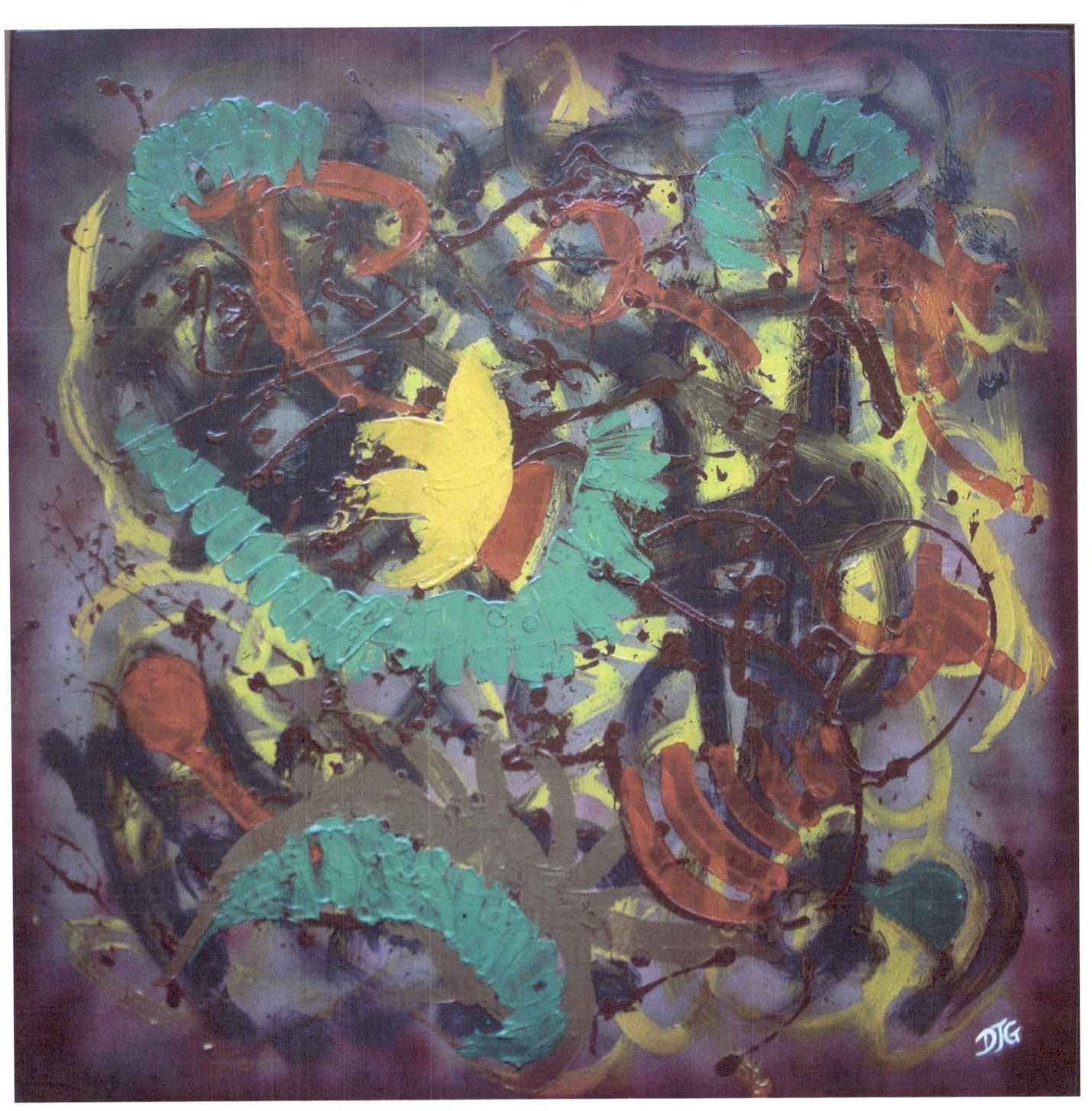

Organic – Acrylic on canvas – 48 x 48"

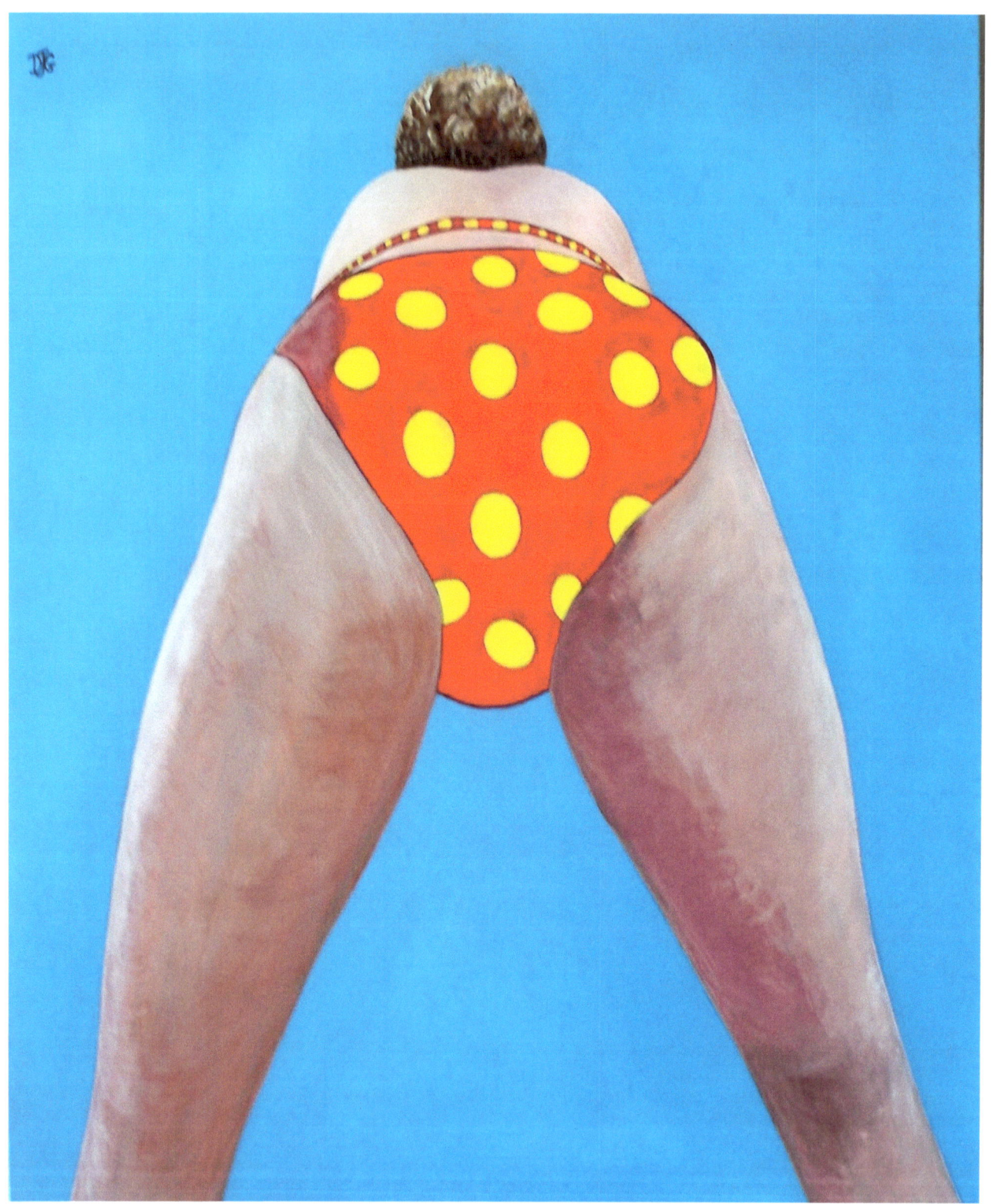

Posterior Projection – Acrylic on canvas – 36" x 36"

All Original Pictures
are available for sale.

FOR ADDITIONAL INFORMATION, CONTACT:

Dr. David J. Goodwill
Telephone: 404-285-5913

or

Email: drdjgoodwill@aol.com